MUSIC FOR ALL

Teaching Music To People With Special Needs

LOIS BIRKENSHAW-FLEMING

CONTENTS

Introduction... v
1 GENERAL IDEAS.. 1
    I   *Teaching Styles and Techniques* 2
    II   *Space and Equipment* 4
    III *Routines* 5
    IV *Choosing Partners and Groups* 6
    V   *Relaxation* 6
    VI *Movement* 7
    VII *Notation* 10
    VIII *Singing* 16
    IX *Instruments* 18
    X   *Teaching Instruments* 24
    XI *Modifications for Instruments, Beaters, and Picks* 30
    XII *Left and Right* 32
    XIII *3/4 and 6/8 Meter* 32
    XIV *Holding Hands* 32
    XV *Puppets, Dolls, and Stuffed Toys* 33
    XVI *Music Appreciation* 33
    XVII *Examinations* 37
    XVIII *Recitals* 38

2 MENTAL DISABILITIES 39
3 PHYSICAL DISABILITIES 47
4 VISUAL DISABILITIES 57
5 HEARING DISABILITIES 69
6 LEARNING DISABILITIES 81
7 AUTISM 91
8 BEHAVIORAL DISORDERS 101
9 SENIORS 105
10 BOOKS, RECORDS, AND TAPES 113
11 USEFUL ADDRESSES 117

INTRODUCTION

OVER the last few decades, people with special needs have become more and more accepted as a part of general society. As a result, people with exceptionalities are participating in activities that were once virtually denied them. Blind people are climbing mountains; physically disabled people are downhill skiing; people with physical and/or mental problems are taking part in special olympics; visually handicapped people are studying art; and more and more people with a wide range of disabilities are studying music.

In recent years, music teachers in the school system have seen increasing numbers of students who have various mental and physical disabilities in their classrooms, and private music teachers are being approached by special-needs students who wish to study music.

Seniors, too, are no longer content to sit back and watch life from the sidelines but are signing up for all kinds of classes and activities (including music lessons) in record numbers. Although most seniors are not disabled, they do have special needs, and in many instances adaptations in content and method of instruction must be made for them. Many seniors interested in music studies wish to learn a new instrument or continue to study an instrument they learned many years ago. Some may wish to join a choir or take a course in music appreciation.

For teachers who are willing to include students with special needs in their teaching schedules, the rewards can be great. The one characteristic these students have in common is their sincere eagerness to learn and their delight in accomplishment – no matter how small.

Along with the rewards there are challenges. Adjustments and changes in the curriculum and sometimes in the physical set-up of the teaching space must often be made to accommodate these students.

Each student is a unique individual with his or her own way and pace of learning. Programs must be adapted to suit the abilities and learning styles of all students. This is especially true for people with exceptionalities, who require programs tailored to their needs in order for them to succeed in music studies.

Most teacher-training programs do not include instruction in working with special-needs students, and the prospect of teaching these individuals without prior knowledge can well be daunting. This book was written to acquaint teachers with the more common disabilities and problems that might be encountered in teaching people with special needs. It also suggests practical ideas, activities, and adaptations that could be used.

The ideas presented here are meant to facilitate music teaching and learning. As music teachers, we are mainly concerned with the affective side of music – imparting a knowledge of music to students and instilling in them a love of music. These aims are usually accomplished by teaching students to play instruments or to sing so that they might explore the wonders of the traditional and modern musical literature and hopefully be able to experience the delight of creating their own music. This study is accompanied by a study of theory – harmony, history, and form. In short, our aim is music education. *Music for All* hopes to help teachers realize this aim.

Many of the activities and suggestions in this book could as easily come under the heading of recreational music, that is, the use of music for sheer enjoyment. For people with special needs, recreational music is tremendously important and can provide a safe place for the development of social skills, the release of emotions, and the satisfaction that comes from making music with others.

Music therapy, on the other hand, uses the elements of music (melody, rhythm, form, dynamics, pitch, and timbre) to help individuals who have emotional, physical, or mental difficulties. Music is used intentionally to bring about a positive change, and the choice of music and activities is governed by this intent. Music therapy contains many elements of recreational music and music education, but healing is its primary aim. Music therapy should never be attempted by persons who are not trained therapists.

This book is intended for the private music teacher working with people of all ages. However, instrumental teachers who work with single pupils or small groups in the schools will also find ideas that will make learning more effective. Classroom teachers are referred to *Come On Everybody, Let's Sing*, published by Gordon V. Thompson Music, which deals more specifically with the school situation.

In addition, *Music for All* may prove valuable to parents and caregivers, whose role in the musical life of the student cannot be overemphasized. Learning an instrument is a lonely business for most children and others too. Parents and caregivers, who are such a large part of the student's life, can be a tremendous help. They can encourage the students, help with practicing, play simple accompaniments to provide a background for the students' beginning melodies, perform echo games by clapping or with percussion instruments, listen to recordings with the students, take them to concerts, and generally participate in their musical life. By offering support and showing that they enjoy music, parents and caregivers will help the student to enjoy music and to overcome the difficulties that inevitably occur in the learning process. This involvement is particularly important for those who have special problems.

The first chapter of *Music for All* contains ideas and suggestions that could be used with a wide variety of exceptionalities. Chapters 2 to 9 deal with specific disabilities and include activities that will facilitate the teaching of students who have these problems. Chapter 10 – "Books, Records, and Tapes," gives suggestions for further sources of information, while Chapter 11 contains lists of addresses of various organizations (to consult for further information and help) and places to obtain materials.

Thanks are due to many people – friends, relatives, colleagues, and students – for their help in the writing of this book. In particular I would like to thank my husband, Kip Fleming, for his patience and wise counsel; James Leahy, my editor, who made so many excellent suggestions; Kathy Bidell and the others at Gordon V. Thompson, who believed in the project from the beginning; and two fellow teachers, Susan Hamblin and David E. Walden, who made many helpful comments on parts of the manuscript.

It is hoped that *Music for All* will assist the teacher and others in planning music experiences for special learners and in understanding their needs. Music should be for everyone; it is hoped that the ideas in this book will help to make that goal come true for a greater number of people.

Lois Birkenshaw-Fleming
January 1993

1   GENERAL IDEAS

● ●

THERE are several general principles and observations that might prove helpful in teaching students who have special needs. The more knowledge you have about the student, the more effective you will be in reaching him or her and the more comfortable you will be with the person. Find out as much as you can about the student's disability by consulting parents, former teachers, counselors, and the students themselves. Read books and articles on the student's particular disability.

Avoid having fixed preconceptions of what people with impairments and disabilities can and cannot do. Often, these opinions have been imposed by over-protective people in the student's past and may not be valid today. Listen to advice, but keep an open mind about your students' potential.

If, in spite of your best efforts, one of your regular students is unable to overcome a particular block (reading notation, for example), you might suspect problems in eye-hand coordination, mirror reading, left-to-right sequencing, and so on. Inquire from the parent if such a difficulty has ever been encountered or ask the student directly (if the student is an adult). Many basic learning difficulties have been uncovered first by music teachers.

Being natural in your conversation will put the student at ease. Do not try to modify your vocabulary by eliminating all references to "seeing, walking, hearing," and so on. For example, to avoid talking about colors to a blind person could seem stilted and awkward.

Always maintain a positive, encouraging attitude. "That chord was wrong" can be just a fact for most students, but for those who have special needs and whose self-esteem is fragile, a statement like this can be devastating and may even result in a complete loss of control. It would be better to say, "That sounded so much better. Let's try it again and use *this* chord," and then show them the proper notes.

Sometimes we are unsure how a student is perceiving the individual notes or how the brain is absorbing the music. Having great patience and presenting the material in as many different ways as possible (using many different learning modalities – visual, aural, kinesthetic, and tactile) seem to lead to the greatest success.

As discussed in the Introduction, music teachers are mostly concerned with the affective side of music. It is important to understand, however, the developmental benefits that can come from participation in musical activities. These benefits include the following:

1. A sense of self-worth can be derived from real accomplishments, large or small. This can be obtained when the student is allowed to proceed at his or her own pace. Competition with others is usually counterproductive and harmful especially for students who have special needs.

   It is also important to maintain the highest possible standards of participation, performance, and musicianship so that the learning achievement will be a valid experience. Of course, these standards will sometimes have to be modified depending on the abilities and disabilities of the individual students. However, everyone must be encouraged to achieve the highest level of which they are capable and to be as independent as possible in music activities as well as in everyday life.
2. Social interaction is encouraged through music activities. This is tremendously important when disabling conditions so often result in isolation.
3. Coordination and motor sensory skills can be developed and muscle strength can be maintained (especially in the case of seniors) by using movement activities with music.
4. When combined with speech activities, music can help students who have difficulties with speech and language production.
5. Music can help develop all facets of listening. These might include listening awareness, auditory discrimination, auditory sequencing, and memory.
6. An active, comprehensive music program uses the whole brain. The affective, intuitive right side of the brain is stimulated along with the more logical, sequential left side to give a more holistic approach to education than is possible with most other subjects.

I GENERAL TEACHING STYLES AND TECHNIQUES

1. Proceed from the known to the unknown in small steps and "chunks." The task is then to make the "unknown" become the

"known." Always begin a lesson with something that is within the student's range of abilities. This builds confidence.

2. Repeat, repeat, repeat. Present the same concept in many different ways so that each person has a chance to absorb it in his or her strongest modality of learning.

   Try to make repetition fun by using some of the following techniques:

   - "Nice try! Let's play it again making the right hand beautifully smooth like syrup."

   - Have some method of keeping track of the number of times a section has been repeated. You could have two boxes, one containing poker chips. After each repetition, a poker chip is transferred to the other box.

   - Guard against meaningless repetition by playing or singing the passage differently each time: left hand only/right hand only, soft/loud, fast/slow, and so on. These directions could be written on cards that are shuffled and performed in the order that the student selects. (Blank decks of cards are available from school supply stores.) If the student cannot read, draw symbols to indicate how the passage is to be played:

3. Keep coming back to songs and music that have been learned previously. This gives the student a sense of security. Everyone can relax and participate in a familiar activity.

4. When using classroom instruments, use only a few at a time, otherwise the sound will be too loud and there will be no listening.

5. Use all the instruments you have brought for each class. Students will be disappointed if some have not been played and will certainly let you know about it.

6. Keep directions simple and clear. Having the students repeat the instructions after you might seem boring, but it will ensure that understanding has taken place.

7. Commands that are sung ("Come to the piano now") rather than spoken are often more effective in getting the student's attention. You can use as few as three notes for these commands. They do not have to be complicated.

8. Use sound as a focusing agent: "When I play this chord, come

and sit at the piano." "Everyone sit down when you hear the tri-angle play."

9. Also good for focusing agents are concrete materials and tactile aids such as pictures; puppets or large dolls; interesting instruments such as maracas, large cymbals, puli pulis, agogo bells (and other instruments from different cultures); notes made from sandpaper; and toy trucks, cars, dinosaurs, and so on. All these items can be manipulated and involve different senses.

10. Plan activities that involve personal choice (for example, sound exploration). This will encourage creativity and independence.

11. Use a hands-on experiential approach. Try to *do*, not *talk*, as much as possible.

12. Use activities and materials that activate several senses: beep balls (balls with small bells inside), brightly colored notes, pull toys that make sounds.

13. Have a quiet way of giving praise for work well done. Noisy, exciting applause is upsetting. Give one big clap or let them pat themselves on the back. "Give Tony one big clap for playing the drum so well." "Daniela, pat yourself on the back. You sang very well today." Be sure to encourage each student in every lesson by praising something he or she has done well. Young children love rewards such as stickers and stars, but, again, make sure each child receives one for doing *something* correctly.

14. If you teach an instrument such as piano on a one-to-one basis, try to involve the students in activities away from the instrument. For example, if the student is having difficulty with the rhythm ♫ ♫ ♩ ♩ │♩ ♩ ♩ 𝄽 and no amount of counting has helped, have the student say a little speech pattern in the rhythm – "We are going out now to the store" or "We like playing baseball every day." Clap the rhythm while saying the speech pattern; play it on a drum or on claves; walk it on the floor. In this way the rhythm becomes part of the whole person and the student is ready to integrate it into the original music. (See also Section X – "Tips for Teaching Instruments.")

15. Plan more activities than you think you will need, in case one activity does not prove to be successful that day. This allows you to be flexible and to respond to the needs of the student(s).

II SPACE AND EQUIPMENT

The space for teaching music should be warm and inviting but not too "busy." Students with certain emotional and learning disabilities can become easily distracted when the environment has many competing colors, pictures, and designs.

1. If you have a class that sits on the floor, have a rug or individual carpet squares for the students to sit on for warmth and comfort.
2. Have a specific place set aside for classroom instruments and equipment. Return these neatly to their proper space each time they are used. Making a diagram of the shape of each instrument and placing this on the shelf or table will encourage the students to put things away in the correct places while at the same time help them learn spatial relationships.
3. If movement activities are part of your lessons, try to teach in a space that is of medium size but large enough for the students to move in without feeling cramped. A space that is too large, on the other hand, tends to cause excitable behavior in some students.
4. Plan to have equipment such as percussion instruments, charts, cassette players, tapes, and so on, ready beforehand. This cuts down on distractions. Nothing loses the attention of a group faster than watching the teacher rummage around in a cupboard for a mallet, a triangle, or a cassette tape.
5. Have a set of unpitched percussion instruments to use as an aid in teaching rhythm patterns. They give a variety of sound and help the students concentrate on the immediate task.
6. A "prop" box with hats, canes, puppets, scarves, pieces of material, and so on, can act as a catalyst for creative drama.
7. Have chairs of the correct height for the students and be prepared with specially adapted tables, mallets, or instrument holders, if your students require these.

III ROUTINES

In a classroom or private teaching studio a fairly set routine will offer security. Many people with mental, emotional, or learning disabilities experience so much disorder and chaos in their lives that they respond well to the sense of order that routines impose.

1. Start and end exactly on time.
2. Have the same greeting, chant, or "hello" song to begin each class.
3. Keep a set plan for each lesson – vary the content but not the general outline.
4. Try not to allow any interruptions such as phone calls to take place during the class.

5. Have a specific plan for getting equipment out and putting it away each lesson. Make sure that this routine is always followed.
6. Establish a way to end the class, for example, a "goodbye" song, a handshake, a special way of saying or chanting goodbye.

IV CHOOSING PARTNERS AND GROUPS WHEN WORKING WITH CLASSES

It saves a great deal of time if the choosing of partners is organized ahead of time. As the group enters the room, give out some means of identification. When the time comes to get into partner formation the students can easily find the person who has the same identifying object as they do. The following are good ideas for matching:

■ scarves of the same color to wear around the wrist or neck;
■ two pieces of cardboard of matching color to wear on a string around the neck;
■ two pieces of paper of the same shape to pin on – triangles, squares, crescents;
■ pictures of the same object to pin on – pumpkins, hearts, flags, guitars, drums;
■ a grown animal and its baby – a horse and a colt, a cow and a calf;
■ one person with Ludwig and the other with van Beethoven, Richard and Wagner, Michael and Jackson.

If you want the class to form groups later in the lesson, give each child a swatch of a color as they come in, then he or she can go quickly to the green corner, the red corner, the yellow corner, and so on.

V RELAXATION

Activities that encourage relaxation are very important for everyone in this hurried, frantic world and are even more important to build into programs for special-needs students. These students are often frustrated by trying to achieve the standards set by society and often have a history of failure to overcome. Tension and anxiety can be the result.

Schedule relaxation activities before the music period begins or between other activities when you sense that the students are becoming tense. Here are a few ideas:

1. Have the students sit on a chair or lie on the floor. Have them close their eyes and listen to the sounds around them. After a

period of time they can open their eyes, and (if lying down) slowly sit up and discuss what they heard.

2. Have everyone get into a comfortable position and listen to some quiet, relaxing music. *Afternoon of a Faun* by Debussy, *Morning Mood* by Grieg, *The Lonely Shepherd* by Zamfir, and *Symphony Number 5*, second movement, by Tchaikovsky are good choices.

    Also try meditation tapes of quiet music such as those by Steven Halpern and Kintaro, or play tapes of the natural sounds of the forest and the sea such as *Solitudes I* and *II* produced by Holborne Records, Toronto. These are all tremendously relaxing.

3. Have older students lie down on mats or cushions and ask them to relax all parts of the body in turn as they are mentioned.

4. Ask the students to stand erect, reach way up to the ceiling, and then let go, flopping over and bending to the floor, hanging loosely. (They should always keep the knees bent to avoid damage to their backs.) Have them slowly come erect, and repeat. Breathe in while reaching up, and out when flopping over.

5. Use appropriate poetry to engender relaxation.

6. Students can imitate things that are limp and relaxed such as jellyfish, old rag dolls, a parachute floating down.

7. Move to gentle music, using light, floating scarves or streamers.

8. Move to gentle music in 3/4 and 6/8 meters (see Section XIII).

9. Try some slow, gentle deep breathing. This makes the whole body relax.

VI MOVEMENT

Movement is a natural part of all learning. It can release tensions, help the body assimilate concepts, lead to social contacts through dancing or sports, and is generally a vital part of all life. Many people with special needs are virtually deprived of this pleasure because of their disabilities, so including some movement activities as a part of all musical learning is even more important for these students. Some general ideas for movement activities follow.

Making a Statue or Shape

As music begins in silence, movement begins in stillness. Making shapes is often a good way to begin movement activities because the attention is focused on the body and the person becomes prepared for movement. Ending a movement activity by making a shape is a good way to give a sense of form and completeness to the exercise. Young children might better understand the concept of making a shape if it is first described as a statue. Here are a few sample instructions:

- "Make a statue (shape). Another one. Another one."
- "Make yourself into a statue that is long and skinny; short and round; one that has jagged edges; the funniest one you can think of."
- "Can you keep your shape and move across the room?"
- "Can you keep your shape and move slowly (or quickly) way up high (down low, in the middle)? Can you start slowly and get faster?"
- "Can you end by making another shape and holding it until you hear the sound of the triangle?"

Non-locomotor Movement

With some students – hyperactive children, those who are afraid of space (some visually impaired, hearing impaired, or emotionally disturbed students), or those who are confined to wheelchairs – it is best to begin movement activities with nonlocomotor exercises. Here are a few suggestions:

- "Stretch your arms way up high, to the sides, to the floor, to the front/back."
- "Bend yourself in as many places as you can. What parts of your body bend?"
- "Twist yourself into knots."
- "Shake yourself out and relax. Shake all parts of your body – head, arms, feet, fingers, shoulders, etc."

Locomotor Activities

- "Move any place in the room, walking at your own speed."
- "Listen to the drum and move the way it tells you to – fast, slow, skipping, jumping."
- "Move in a different direction as the sound of the drum changes."
- Have the students find different ways to walk – on toes/heels, up high, down low, backwards, cross-footed. Students in wheelchairs could "walk" with their hands.
- Challenge the students to find many different ways to walk, run, skip, and jump. This exercises their imaginations. Attaching jingle bells to wrists or ankles will enable the students to hear the rhythms of movement as well as to perform them.

■ Join several different movements into a short sequence – for example, walk four steps, turn one time, jump two times (large jumps), and squat on heels.

Springboards into Movement

Many students need an impetus to encourage movement. This might involve using movement to dramatize a poem or story, imitate a machine or animal, or describe the texture of different items such as stones, light silk scarves, or water. Activities that use lummi sticks or parachutes or different-sized balls are very useful especially when you are working with special-needs students.

Dancing

Try movement activities that involve dancing. These might be folk dances, social dances, games and dances created for songs, or creative dances that the students have devised.

Certain formations work best for students of different ages. *Scatter formation*, in which each person dances on his or her own is best for young children or students who do not relate well to others. *Circles* give security (there are people on each side and everyone can see everyone else). *Lines* encourage more independent movement. *Partners* involve one-to-one interaction. Many people may not be ready for partner formations for quite a long time.

The following are some ideas to help make *all* dancing work smoothly:

■ Walk and talk through the dances first, describing the movements as you perform them. This helps learning.

■ Have some way (colors, scarves, etc.) of indicating partners (see Section IV).

■ Don't have the students hold hands if there is resistance to this. Blind people, particularly blind children, do not like to have their hands immobilized.

■ Students in wheelchairs can perform many of the dances with their upper bodies or in their chairs. Make sure there is enough space for this. There has been a great deal of interest in wheelchair dancing in recent years, particularly in England. Groups have been formed, several books on the topic have been written, and conventions have been held for people who enjoy this activity (see Chapter 10 – "Books, Records, and Tapes" for a list of books on wheelchair dancing).

VII NOTATION

Many students who have special needs are capable of learning traditional notation easily. For others, such as visually impaired students or those with severe learning disabilities, other means of conveying musical ideas must be found such as braille or learning by rote or from a cassette. Seniors might resist learning to read notes and prefer to play by ear. Some students require alternate learning approaches to unlock the mysteries of note reading. The following are a few of these approaches.

Iconic Representation

Music is one of the most abstract of languages, and many people with special needs learn only when concrete ideas such as pictures or symbols (iconic representation) are used to present information:

Concepts such as crescendo ⟨⟨⟨ fast/slow 𝖬𝖬𝖬𝖬𝖬\/\/\ high/low ☼ ⟨⟨⟨⟨⟨⟨⟨⟨⟨ can be shown in pictures (i.e., This melody goes up ⤴ . This melody goes down ⤵ .).

Traditional Note Values

1. Introduce note values when the student is able to comprehend them in terms of movement. For example: walking ♩ ♩ ♩ ♩ ; then running ♫ ♫ ♫ ♫ . When the student can jump, or walk, stop and wait, then introduce ♩ ♩ . Finally introduce other notes. Each step should be carefully timed and should build on previous learning and on developmental readiness.

    Students who cannot walk or run may be able to show a kinesthetic understanding by walking, running, or jumping with their fingers on a tabletop.

2. When the students know their note values well, write a measure of these values on cards and play games that will help to drill the concept:

    ■ Put the cards face down on the floor in a circle. The students walk anywhere in the room to a drumbeat. When the music stops they stand behind one of the cards, turn it over, and at the teacher's signal, clap, patsch, snap, or stamp their note value(s) for four measures. Repeat the game.

    ■ Make this game more difficult by mixing up the note values and creating rhythm patterns; by using syncopation; by making the patterns longer; by using dotted rhythms, sixteenth notes, mixed meter – whatever is appropriate for the students.

- The same game can be played using notes written on a staff. The students have to identify these and/or sing them. Have a small xylophone or piano available to give the correct pitch of the first note.

3. Use large and small circles to show beat and accent:

These could be translated into traditional rhythmic notation at a later date if the students are ready.

4. Words and pictures can also be used to show rhythms and accents:

$$\bigcirc \quad \bigcirc \quad \bigcirc\bigcirc \quad \bigcirc \qquad ☆☆ \quad ☆ \quad ☆☆ \quad ☆$$
ball, ball, little ball   little star,   little star

5. Show note values by using different lengths of lines. Make sure that the relationships are exactly correct (i.e., the quarter note length is two times longer than the eighth note; the half note is two times longer than the quarter note, and so on). Make a set of these from pieces of half-inch-square wood or from coffee stir sticks cut to the proper lengths, and let the students create rhythm patterns. They can then clap or play these on a drum.

6. Make notes from Plasticine, sandpaper, raised lines on cards, with round felt circles, coffee stir sticks, or in other ways that involve the sense of touch and the manipulation of material.

7. Play musical bingo. Each person has a card filled with rhythms instead of numbers. When the leader claps a rhythm and a person has this rhythm, he or she covers that square with a marker. Again, this game could be played using individual notes written on a staff, or musical terminology (i.e., crescendo, ritard, allegro, and so on). For this latter game, the leader would give the definitions and the students would match these with the correct word.

Key Signatures and Scales

Some students can learn to read music by having the whole scheme of keys and key signatures presented in logical, chordal progression: C+

chord changing to C7 and going to F+; F+ chord changing to F7 and going to B flat; and so on. Continue on through the flat side of the "key circle," make the enharmonic change, and come back through the sharp side, ending with G7 moving to C+. This neat progression often takes the mystery out of key signatures for many people.

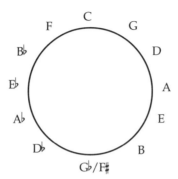

Many of these same people find it a satisfying challenge to work out all the major scales at the keyboard using the tone–tone–semitone formula. Scales then make sense because the arrangement of the whole and half tones is always in the same order no matter what note you start with. Once the concept is understood, the writing of scales can be introduced. Use large-sized manuscript paper to make it easier. (This can be produced on copying machines that have a device for enlarging the original.)

Other Ways of Presenting Notation

Make a large staff by painting it (with special fabric paints) on a long piece of white cloth. This can be placed on the floor, and students can add the notes, staff signs, key signatures, and so on. The students themselves can move to the correct place in response to the names of the notes called out by the teacher, or they can become the notes by stepping from spaces to lines to create a melody for themselves.

Metal boards can be painted white or covered with white Mactac. Staves can then be painted on the surface. Use black, round magnets for notes and strips of black, magnetic tape for the stems. This magnetic tape can also be fixed to the backs of notes, sharps, clefs, and so on, that have been made from thick cardboard.

Music Education Systems manufactures a large plastic board with the keyboard printed on it. An optional board shows the treble clef above and the bass clef below. The keyboard starts with the note A and the system uses the normal alphabet right from the beginning. This device is successful because the students can see the logic in it. The letter names of the keys or the correct fingering to be used can be written right on the board with a dry-erase marker. The notes are two inches wide and are easy to see and comprehend. The same company sells sets of 13″ × 22″ plastic student boards and a rhythm kit containing plastic cards with different note values. Teachers and students can use these cards to create their own rhythm patterns. Because the size of the cards matches the duration of each note value, rhythms can be taught in a visual, logical, and sequential way that always stresses the relationships and beat groupings. See Chapter 11 – "Useful Addresses" for information on ordering these materials.

Use extra-large manuscript paper and fat, easy-to-hold crayons to draw with. In particular, young children and students who have poor motor coordination will find it easier to work with large scores and large crayons.

These methods of presenting notation make it easier for some special-needs students to comprehend the concepts because they are using manipulable, hands-on materials that make everything more concrete and involve many learning modalities.

Play games in which the students have to complete sentences by deciphering the names of notes written on the staff (substitute notes written on the staff for the words in capitals when writing this out for students):

When I took a trip on the train my BAGGAGE was lost. I hoped that some BAD person had not taken it. I went in a CAB to the lost and found office and was told that I had to wait so I went to the store and bought some BEEF and some CABBAGE. Back at the lost and found I found one BAG in a CAGE and the other on the EDGE of the counter. I FACED the attendant, gave him a FEE, and took a CAB to a CAFE and ordered an EGG. When I got home I was DEAD tired.

Computer-Assisted Learning

There are several computer programs that link an electronic keyboard to a staff that appears on the computer screen. Whatever is played is entered on the score – melodies, single notes, key signatures, chords, and so on. One of these programs, Practica Musica (which runs on Macintosh computers), also teaches basic theory. Melodies can be created, and chords and other parts added. Everything can be changed as the student wishes and printed out on paper when the piece of music is complete. For older students this is an excellent way to link sound and notation.

Note-reading programs are fairly complicated, so the teacher might have to devise ways of teaching the very basic concepts before using the commercial products. Encore and Finale are two programs that have been particularly successful with older students and adult learners who are able to work at their own pace. This method has been popular in high schools and community colleges where the students are at different levels of musical competence.

Color-Coding Notes

Some students can achieve success in playing melodies if the notes are color coded. Buy commercially produced, round, colored stickers or make your own with masking tape and magic markers. Put the stickers right on the notes of the keyboard and color the notes or circle them in the corresponding color in the manuscript.

Another idea is to put a sticker on a note and a sticker of the same color on the finger that will play the note.

I find it wise to use to the colors most commonly used on little xylophones:

C – red
B – violet
A – indigo
G – sky blue
F – green
E – yellow
D – orange
C – red

Relate these to the colors of the rainbow. If your students confuse sky blue, indigo, and violet, you might substitute a contrasting color such as brown or black for the A (indigo).

Charts for Chord Reading

Charts can assist students in playing chords to accompany songs or instrumental melodies. These charts can be made in various ways depending on the user's level of competence. For example:

- Chord symbols:

I	I	V	V
I	IV	V	I

- Letter names:

D	D	A	A
D	G	A	D

- Color and shape coded:

●	●	▲	▲
●	■	▲	●

Giving each note a different shape as well as a different color will aid in differentiation. This is particularly important if the students are color blind.

Small pieces of tape marked with the corresponding symbols and stuck to the keys of instruments can help students find the correct notes and chords.

Shapes, Stickers, Numbers, and Letters

Some teachers have had success using shapes, stickers, or pictures of different animals or toys to represent the notes. Some of these schemes can become rather complicated, but the beauty of the method is that it focuses the students' attention on the individual notes and the fingers that will play them.

Sheila Mofson has developed a system that uses shapes for the individual notes of the C scale:

These shapes tend to lessen the confusion in distinguishing notes and intervals and help the student to read efficiently. Gradually, these shapes are replaced with traditional notation. (See Chapter 11 – "Useful Addresses" for information on how to order this method.)

Giving each note a number is also a popular method; in fact, whole courses of study have been written using numbers. The disadvantage of this system is that the student will eventually have to unlearn it and switch to letters. It is perhaps best to start with letters at the outset (if your students can read them). Many teachers find that using capital letters to replace or add to regular notation is helpful in teaching students with special needs to "read music." The letter system works particularly well when teaching recorder, violin, or other instruments that play a single melody line.

Letters and numbers have an advantage in that they avoid the use of the staff. Depicting the rhythm is tricky in these methods, so it is usually taught by rote.

"London Bridge" could be:

```
G  A  G  F  E  F  G  –    or    5  6  5  4  3  4  5  –
D  E  F  –  E  F  G  –          2  3  4  –  3  4  5  –
```

Have the students draw their notes on large scores, which are easier to read and require less fine motor coordination.

The students could create their own melodies right from the start, even when they know only very few notes. Wanting to find a way to preserve their "compositions" will encourage students to learn some form of notation.

Always relate the sound to the notes by playing "melodies" or individual notes on a piano, recorder, violin, or other instrument.

No one method will be successful with every student. Try many until you find the one best suited to the individual needs of each person. Always try to get as near as possible to traditional notation. Think of the ways of showing notation as a continuum, with iconic representation at one end, working through long and short lines, numbers and/or capital letters and so on, up to regular notation. Move the students as far as they are able along this scale toward traditional note reading.

If, in spite of your best efforts, the student is still unable to learn notation, take heart – many people, such as Paul McCartney, have been able to achieve success in the music world without being able to read music.

VIII SINGING

Most people love to sing, and people with special needs are no exception. Although the resulting sound may resemble more a "joyful noise" than a melody, this should not discourage teacher or student.

Even if the student is studying an instrument with fixed tuning, such as piano or organ, singing the music will give him or her a better feeling of line and shape. For those who are studying stringed instruments or certain woodwinds and brass, singing the melody will help their intonation. Being comfortable with singing helps the student project the emotions of the music.

The following ideas will help improve the quality of the sound even though it might never reach perfection. Do not try too many of these ideas at one time. Concentrate on only one or two per session.

1. Good posture is absolutely essential for good singing. (It can also help students play instruments more effectively and without muscle strain.)
2. Make sure the students open their mouths wide enough to allow the sound to come out.
3. Taking good, deep breaths can greatly improve the quality of sound and also aids lung development.
4. "Open your eyes!" and "Smile with your eyes!" are prompts that will help the student project the voice better.
5. Have the students listen to the other singers in the group. This is a particularly good idea if a student is singing too loudly.
6. Have the student or group sing the first note with you to make sure they are in tune at the beginning.
7. To encourage in-tune singing, do "Questions and Answers" (call and response) and echo work with the group. These can be be sung to as few as three notes and are a great help in keeping the singing on pitch. For example: "Marcia are you here?" "Yes I am." "Derek, did you come to choir on the subway?" "No I got a ride with Paul."
8. Sing songs with fairly easy words about subjects that interest the students.
9. Try songs that use repetition in words and music. Songs with repeated choruses are good.
10. Keep the pitch low enough to be comfortable for the majority of singers in the group. Many people with special needs sing with low voices.
11. The range should not be too great, nor should there be many difficult leaps.
12. Songs with actions or movement are popular.
13. Write easy words to familiar melodies. The students then will have to learn only the words. *Piggy Back Songs* and *More Piggy Back Songs* by Jean Warren have some wonderfully inventive suggestions (see Chapter 10 – "Books, Records, and Tapes").
14. With older groups try scat singing. Traditional neutral vowel sounds such as "dooby, doo" and "baa, baa be bap" are fun and easy to pronounce.
15. Try making up rap songs. These are easy and are a good introduction to the art of singing (especially for out-of-tuners) because they use very few tones and have a strong rhythmic component.

16. It might be desirable to integrate students with special needs into a regular singing group or choir. Make sure these people have opportunities to learn the music away from the group so that they will experience success when taking part with everyone. Position special-needs students near strong singers (who can help them along) and designate one person to be a "buddy" who can help them keep their place in the music and give signals when to leave the stage, when to begin singing, and so on.

For more books on the development of vocal technique and/or good choir work, see Chapter 10 – "Books, Records, and Tapes."

IX INSTRUMENTS

Young children should be given the opportunity to explore freely a variety of sound-makers – those found around the home (such as mixing bowls, flower sifters, suspended pot lids, macaroni on a string, a comb scraped with a pencil) and the more traditional classroom and orchestral instruments. Older students also enjoy experimenting with different ways of producing sounds from a variety of sources, but these sound sources have to be more sophisticated. Electronic keyboards can produce a tremendous variety of sounds with just a touch of a button and are wonderful for developing sound awareness. Be careful not to have too many choices available because this may stimulate hyperactive behavior.

As the students gain experience, some of the exploration can be directed: "Can you play a loud sound?" "Can you make your sound loud at first, then slowly make it go very soft?" "Can you join with another person and put your two sounds together in some way?" In this way a sense of form is developed and cooperation is encouraged.

Hand Percussion (Unpitched) Instruments

These instruments come in all shapes, sizes, and sounds and from all parts of the world. Some of the most useful include hand drums, claves, bells (jingle bells, ceramic bells, wooden bells), cymbals and gongs, shakers (very easy for students to make themselves), tambourines, maracas, and castanets.

They can be used to create rhythmic solos or to accompany recorded music by keeping the beat or playing a rhythmic pattern. They are also useful for developing rhythmic awareness and in creating sound effects for poems or stories and for accompanying movement.

If the students are playing unpitched percussion instruments in groups, charts can be prepared to indicate just where they come in:

✕ = Sticks   ◯ = Drum   = Tambourine   = Cymbal

Melodic Percussion Instruments

Xylophones, metallophones, and glockenspiels are very easy to play, sound musically pleasing, and have removable bars to make it even easier for the special-needs student to achieve success. Ensembles can quickly come together, each person playing a short, repeated pattern (ostinato) with the final result sounding very "full" musically.

Carl Orff's *Music for Children* is an approach to teaching that uses these instruments. The first songs and melodies in this method use two, three, and finally, five notes (the pentatonic scale). These can be accompanied easily by instruments set up in the same key. The basic accompaniment is the bordun (notes 1 and 5) played over and over. The next is the ostinato, which consists of 3 notes (in 3/4 time) or 4 notes (in 4/4 time) – still in the pentatonic scale. These are repeated over and over. I have found that ostinatos are most successful if one of the notes is the key note; but given this small restriction, students can still create their own ostinatos, put them together, combine them with a bordun, and create a full-sounding accompaniment for a song or instrumental melody.

Later on, students can create accompaniments using diatonic melodies that require harmonic changes.

For further suggestions concerning accompaniments and techniques, see Chapter 10 – "Books, Records, and Tapes."

A teacher of piano or other solo instruments might consider adding several pitched and unpitched percussion instruments to his or her studio to create another sound dimension and to facilitate the teaching of rhythm, especially for special-needs students.

Keyboard Instruments

The *piano* is the most useful and accessible keyboard instrument. In addition to being played in the traditional way for solos and accompaniments, the piano can also be used to create sound effects for poems and stories. Even very disabled students can do this.

The drawback of the piano for many students with special needs is that it requires the coordination of both hands (and feet) and a fair degree of strength and dexterity in the fingers. Reading from two lines of music at the same time is sometimes an impossible task for people who have learning disabilities.

The *organ* can produce a wide range of wondrous sounds, some with intense vibrations that can be felt by people with severe hearing disabilities. Some special-needs people, however, will experience complete frustration in playing the traditional instrument and trying to coordinate hands and feet (see Section X).

Electronic organs and keyboards have made it much easier to learn keyboard playing. Even students with severely deformed hands can play melodies and chords on these instruments. Complicated music can be divided into several simple parts that can be played by individual students. On some models, rhythmic accompaniments are available at the touch of a button. Many of these instruments allow the student to create a melody and play it (however slowly) on the keyboard. It can then be retrieved and played back at a faster tempo without a change in key. Some models have a device that will create a chord when only one note is played.

Electronic keyboards can be combined with digital drum systems and other equipment through a MIDI interface to provide great satisfaction and enjoyment for all students. These instruments also lend themselves to group work. The students can all be hooked up to a central mike where they receive instruction from the teacher, or they can be split up into smaller groups where they can learn and create cooperatively on their own.

If sequencers are used, many different instrumental and vocal parts can be recorded one by one on different tracks, as slowly as needed. In this way students are able to compose quite complicated music and experience the thrill of creativity.

Electronic keyboards have many sound effects built into the keyboard. Students can explore these easily and combine them to create interesting sound compositions.

For students with physical disabilities, keyboard stands are adjustable and can fit neatly over wheelchairs for ease of playing (see also Section XI).

Digital pianos are really electronic keyboards but are engineered to approximate the same touch and sound as an acoustic piano. Many models have features that make playing and learning music more interesting and accessible. Here are a few of these features:

1. *Disk drive.* Many of the more elaborate instruments have a disk drive built in, but separate plug-in modules are available for other models. This feature allows access to the extensive libraries of tutorial software. Some programs allow the student to hear the right and left hands separately so that they can practice either one; other disks contain complete keyboard methods such as the Alfred Piano Music Course and the Royal Conservatory of Music series. With some programs you can make the tempo slower (without changing the key) to practice the difficult parts. Some have a playback feature so the student can hear exactly what she or he has played.

   A teacher can prerecord an accompaniment and the student(s) can play or sing with it. This is excellent for working with violin classes or choirs and is also helpful in making the endless repetition of simple material more exciting for the beginning student.

   The software also has recordings of many selections of music that can be used for learning purposes. The solo part can be switched off so the student can play along with the orchestra.

2. *Transposer.* This device transposes the piece being played into another key, making it much easier to change keys when you are working with a group of singers who are unable to sing in the range in which the song has been written.

3. Some models include a built-in *multitrack performance memory* that allows you to add several instrumental parts to build more complicated pieces of music.

4. *Rhythm accompaniment.* The higher-priced models let you back up melodies with bass and chordal patterns. This device is very useful for people who have a disability in the left hand.

5. *External earphones.* These allow for private practice – useful in apartments and for late-night practice.

6. Other features are portability and the fact that the digital piano never goes out of tune.

Ensemble playing becomes easy and fun when several of these instruments are combined. When a computer is introduced into the system, memory capacity is increased and a music-writing program can be employed. Play the notes, hear them, see them on the screen, and print them out. Magic!

The two largest companies in the electronic instrument field are Yamaha and Roland. They both make keyboards, electronic guitars, drum systems, and many other instruments. Instruments from many different manufacturers can be combined through MIDI (Multi Instrument Digital Interface – the internationally accepted interlinking system) and used together.

Digital pianos include the Clavinova (Yamaha) and the Roland piano. Both companies have extensive libraries of software (unfortunately not compatible) and continue to bring out refinements each year. Watch for a voice-activated system!

Ukuleles and Guitars

These popular instruments can be played in the traditional way if the student has sufficient coordination. The use of a capo will allow the student to play in different keys while using the same fingering that was learned for the basic key.

Tuning the strings to produce one chord (for example, D major or C major on the guitar) will allow the students to strum the open strings and accompany pentatonic melodies in that key. Pressing a hard, round object against the strings, such as a small bottle or piece of pipe, will give other chords without the student having to refinger. For example, in D tuning (strings tuned to D, F sharp, and A), the chord of A major (V) can be played by pressing down at the 7th fret and G major (IV) at the 5th fret. The strings of the ukulele can be tuned in a similar way.

Ukuleles and guitars can be restrung "backwards" for students who have dexterity in the right hand but not the left. Holders and clamps can be used to enable the student to grasp picks and strummers. Students with artificial hands can still use these hands to strum or hold picks.

Autoharps and Omnichords

These instruments are used mainly for accompaniment, although the Autoharp can also be a solo instrument. The Omnichord is an electronic version of an Autoharp and will not go out of tune – a distinct advantage since tuning the Autoharp is difficult. Two people can play these instruments, one strumming and the other pressing the buttons to change the chords. Make a stand, or prop the instrument up in some way so it is held at an angle facing the student. It will be much easier to strum. Color or shape coded charts for accompanying chords can be made for greater ease of reading (see Section VII).

Resonator Bells and Handbells

Handbells and resonator bells have been very successful for working with special-needs students. Melodies can be played, accompaniments worked out, and rhythm patterns practiced using just one or two notes. The bells can be divided among several people with each student responsible for one note. Simple individual arrangements can be combined to provide a rich, complete sound. Make charts for the students to follow and color code these if necessary (see Section VII in this chapter and Chapter 2 under "Instruments").

If the students have difficulty playing the traditional handbells they might be able to manage the new tubular ones that have external ringers and do not require as much control.

Recorder

This instrument is fairly easy to play at the beginning, although it is a serious instrument that takes years to master. Much fine and difficult music has been written for the recorder. Recorders are useful for certain special-needs students because they help develop breath control. Many songs can be played on the recorder with just one hand (for the upper notes). Some of these are: "Merrily We Roll Along," "When the Saints Come Marching In," and "Hot Cross Buns."

The recorder is also a very "social" instrument. Many duets, trios, and other ensemble pieces have been written for recorder, and it is easy to arrange music for two or three parts that students can play at an early age and basic level.

Stands can be built to hold the instruments at the correct height so that the student has only to worry about fingering the notes. There is also a one-handed recorder available from Schott, London (see Chapter 11 – "Useful Addresses").

Band and Orchestral Instruments

A knowledge of the traditional instruments of the orchestra and their sounds is important for all students to have, even if they do not plan to study any of them in depth. For special-needs students this knowledge can lead to a lifelong interest in and appreciation of the world of music – classical, popular, and jazz. With the advent of the cassette player, music is accessible to even the most handicapped person and can help to make his or her life more pleasurable.

Recordings such as the *Bowmar Orchestral Library*, *The Carnival of the Animals* (Saint-Saëns), *Peter and the Wolf*, and *Tubby the Tuba* will help to introduce the students to the instruments; however, try as much as possible to let them experiment with and hear the actual sounds of the instruments themselves.

When it comes time to choose an instrument to play, single-reed woodwinds as well as certain brass and percussion instruments are often the best choices for students with special needs. These instruments give more instant gratification than do strings and do not depend as much on a good sense of spatial relationships and relative pitch to play in tune. Instruments to consider are the B-flat soprano clarinet, alto clarinet, alto and tenor saxophone, B-flat trumpet, valve trombone (the slide trombone needs a highly developed sense of spatial relationships), the small upright baritone horn, and the small upright tuba.

Stands will help the students play more easily, as will the use of color coding on the trumpet valves. With patient, highly organized and repetitive teaching, success can be obtained.

Violins, violas, and cellos can be restrung "backwards" so that students can finger with the right hand if the left does not have dexterity. Adaptations can be made using clamps or some other type of holder so the bow can be grasped with a hand that is crippled or even with an artificial hand.

Change fingering patterns to avoid using fingers that have no strength or cannot be controlled.

Orchestral arrangements can be simplified or one part can be divided between two people. These parts could be played first on a tape so that the students will be able to learn them at home by rote.

There are many examples of successful bands made up almost exclusively of people with special needs.

X TEACHING INSTRUMENTS

General

1. *Rote Learning.* Many people have had success in teaching instruments to students with special needs (and others as well) by using the technique of rote learning. Echo play is the foundation of rote learning. The teacher begins by playing one note on an instrument in a simple rhythm and having the student repeat the pattern. The number of notes and the rhythms used are made progressively more complicated and difficult. This sequence could be transferred to a cassette so the student can practice at home. Longer phrases, individual parts (left hand, right hand), and whole sections of the music can be recorded in this way for the student's home use. This, of course, takes hours.

One solution is to record just your part during the lesson, then turn off the recorder while the student echoes, leaving a blank on the tape to be filled in during the student's home practice.

Learning by rote is often more successful than starting with a system that uses notation immediately. The rote method gives instant gratification and develops a keener ear. Blowing, bowing, and strumming techniques can also be learned this way (see Chapter 4, under "Learning Music," for further ideas).

Rote learning is an extension of echo clapping, singing, and playing, which are widely used in the Orff approach, and in other methods, to build good listening skills and rhythmic sureness.

The Suzuki method emphasizes listening. Every piece the student will learn is recorded on cassettes, and each student is required to listen to this music (and the music he or she will learn in future lessons) for hundreds of hours. Many teachers of special-needs students report good success using this method for Book I. However, when the reading begins (at the beginning of Book II), the troubles often begin as well.

The Yamaha Music Education System is another approach to learning music that emphasizes training the ear before introducing notation. There are courses designed for adult beginners, but the most popular are the junior music courses for four- to seven-year-olds. Yamaha stresses that children should be given training in music early (as do other approaches such as Orff, Kodály, Suzuki, and Dalcroze). The Yamaha learning sequence is listening, then singing, then playing. If the student is having difficulty learning notation, the aural approach used at the beginning might have to be extended throughout the whole course.

Perhaps the answer is to try teaching notation by more untraditional means (see Section VII) or to continue teaching by rote. Different solutions will have to be found for each person. Whatever method you use, be aware that learning by rote will play a large part in any approach.

2. *Question and Answer (Phrase Completion).* Question and Answer, or phrase completion, can follow echo work. It is an excellent way to encourage improvisation. The teacher plays a little rhythmic and/or melodic motif and the student responds with a different motif to complete the phrase. You should limit the number of notes used at first and keep the rhythms simple. If you are working on keyboards, use only the black keys at first. This is an easy way to set limits and

ensure success, since these are the notes of a pentatonic scale (in F-sharp major) and any combination will sound fine. After a while, use white keys in different combinations, and finally a blend of white and black. Playing Question and Answer in different registers, up and down the keyboard, will make the students familiar with the entire range of keyboard sounds.

The teacher can accompany echo and question and answer exercises by playing a simple bordun throughout or creating a background of simple chord changes. This establishes the beat and makes things more interesting.

3. *Learning Specific Difficult Passages.* To learn a specific section of a piece that is giving difficulty, repeat it in as many ways as possible using different learning modalities. It often helps to take the student away from the instrument entirely and try some other approaches.

Rhythm:
■ Have the students listen to the rhythm clapped by the teacher.
■ Have them clap the rhythm or tap it on a knee, tray of a wheelchair, or table.
■ Help them find words that would fit the rhythmic pattern. Clap the rhythm and say the words. For example:

Cherry jam,   cherry   jam,   I like bread and cherry jam

■ Walk the rhythm.
■ Play the rhythm on small drums, woodblocks, and/or claves. (Any of these instruments would be useful to have in the studio.) Sometimes it helps if the teacher first plays the rhythm on the instrument that is being held by the student who can then feel the vibrations.
■ Finally, try the rhythmic passage in the context of the whole piece of music.

Melody:
■ Play the melody so the students can hear how it should sound.
■ Have them follow the contour of the melody, moving their hands up and down with it.

- Ask them to draw a "map" of the melody.
- Have them hum along with the melody.
- Can they sing the melody to "lah," either alone or with one or two others?
- Have them go back to the instrument and try to play the melody.

Piano and Other Keyboard Instruments

There are about as many beginning piano and keyboard methods as there are piano teachers. Many of these methods proceed rapidly through the concepts, so the teacher will have to devise supplementary exercises to drill different concepts when working with special-needs students. The following is a description of some well-known approaches.

Music for Piano (Robert Pace). This method uses a multiple-key approach in which the student plays in many keys and ranges up and down the entire keyboard right from the first lessons. This approach also encourages ear training, creative work, and harmonization from very early on. Pace emphasizes (as do many others) the need to prepare the piece "in the air" – playing the piece either on a tabletop or in the air.

Bastien Piano Basics (James and Jane Bastien) and *Alfred's Basic Piano Library* (Willard Palmer, Morton Manus, and Amanda Vick Lethco) use a gradual, multiple-key approach, and both are excellent. *Alfred's Basic Adult Piano Course* is particularly useful for older beginners.

The Music Tree (Frances Clark and Louise Goss) uses the "landmark" approach in which, for example, the student works with all the groups of two black keys together on the keyboard, then all the groups of three black keys and so on. Little melodies with suitable and intelligent words have been written to drill each concept, and interesting accompaniments are provided for the teacher to keep the beat steady and provide musical interest.

The Suzuki Course for piano is very structured and might have to be modified for students with learning difficulties. This method's emphasis on listening and parental involvement is excellent and worth adopting into any teaching plan.

The *Yamaha Music Education System* also emphasizes listening and parental involvement, but may have to be presented in a more flexible way and at a slower pace to accommodate the student who has special needs.

Steven Brown, Sheila Mofson, and Flora Silini have each written piano courses for people with special needs. Mofson uses a system of "shaped" notes to aid in discrimination between tones (see page 15). Silini uses folk material that includes a lot of repetition. Her method stresses preparation away from the piano and paces the introduction of note values and counting time through the clapping of rhythmic chants. This approach would be suitable for a multi-keyboard setup. Unfortunately her book is out of print and is very difficult to find.

Whatever the approach used, the teacher of the special-needs student will have to adapt the materials to suit the particular needs of the students.

Some problems that might arise (particularly when teaching students who have learning disabilities) are:

- The student might have difficulty coordinating both hands.
- The notes of the piece might be correct while the rhythm is wrong, and the student often does not hear that there is a problem.
- The rhythm might be correct while the notes are wrong (and, again, the student remains blissfully oblivious.)
- The student might try to play the left-hand part with the right hand and vice versa.
- The melody may be played correctly but the fingering might change each time the piece is played.
- The fingering and note sequence might be correct but the student has placed her or his hand on the wrong beginning note so that the melody is in the wrong key. Sometimes students do not hear the problem even when the left hand is playing the accompaniment in the correct key at the same time.

The following are a few ideas that might help teaching proceed more smoothly. Many learning modalities can be used to express each concept.

1. Be sure that any printed material for use by the students is clear and free from fussy, distracting illustrations and colors.
2. Prepare the student beforehand (away from the instrument) for the musical concept about to be studied. For example,

    - Clap the rhythm and count out loud using whichever method you wish:

♩	one	taa	walk
♩ ♩	one and	ti-ti	run-ning
♩	one two	taa-aa	walk hold
o	one two three four	taa-aa-aa-aa	walk hold hold hold

You can also use other words that fit the note values as long as you are consistent.

- "Play" little phrases from the music on a tabletop or on an individual printed keyboard. This idea is particularly useful when working with groups of students.
- "Play" the selection up in the air.
- Finally transfer it to the actual keyboard.

3. A flexible and relaxed wrist technique, so necessary for playing keyboard instruments, can be encouraged by developing mallet techniques on melodic percussion instruments. The students can practice keeping the beat to songs, poems, or instrumental pieces by patting their knees lightly with their hands held in a slightly curved position and with very loose wrists. Next, have them "keep the beat" in the air and then play two notes on the xylophone holding mallets. If the xylophone is set up in the pentatonic scale, any notes played will sound pleasing. If the student plays a drone (see below) this can become an accompaniment for a pentatonic song or a pentatonic melody played on a recorder in the same key.

4. Playing drones or bordurs (notes 1 and 5 in a given key) can introduce the student to the wonders of playing keyboards. The teacher can improvise a top part, and immediately the student feels he or she is helping to make music. It is best to confine the improvisation to the pentatonic scale at first (using 1, 2, 3, 5, and 6 of the scale) to avoid dissonances. Play these drones in all keys and in all positions, high and low, to familiarize the student with the whole range of the keyboard. Eventually the student will be able to improvise the melody while the teacher plays the drone. Of course, the next step is for the student to play both drone and melody at the same time.

   When the students start to improvise their own melodies, have them start with the black keys – the pentatonic scale of F-sharp major. In this way, success is ensured from the beginning.

5. Because it is difficult for many special-needs students to do more than one thing at a time, it is sometimes best to have them learn one hand of a piece of music alone for several weeks. Then they can learn the other hand and finally try to put the two together.

   "Mirror" playing, which begins with both thumbs and gradually extends to the other fingers, is often successful because the student employs the same finger of each hand. This is easier for the brain than trying to send signals to two different fingers.

Next, the hands can play in unison, then, finally, the two hands each play something different. Proceed slowly.

Again, it is difficult to make hard and fast rules when teaching special-needs students. However, it is important that the student start playing with both hands as soon as possible. When he or she has begun to read music, learning to read "between the lines," or "in the middle of the staves," helps develop fluency in sight reading. Playing with both hands will help foster this fluency.

6. To teach the curved hand position, which is essential for much piano playing, have the student curve his or her hands around rubber balls of the appropriate size and then have them imagine they are still holding the ball when they play.
7. Another helpful procedure is to have the student place his or her hands directly on top of the teacher's hand as the teacher plays a note. The next step could be for the student to direct the teacher's finger action with his or her own fingers.
8. Squeezing a handful of Plasticine, Silly Putty, or a rubber ball, away from the keyboard, will help build strength. Flexibility can be developed by opening and closing the hands very quickly several times and extending the fingers as far as they will go.

XI MODIFICATIONS FOR INSTRUMENTS, BEATERS, AND PICKS

For students with motor disabilities, slight modifications can be made either to the instruments, the mallets, the strummers, or in the positioning of the player or instrument. The following is a description of some of these modifications. See Chapter 11 – "Useful Addresses" for information on ordering some of the commercial products listed here.

Pedal Extensions

Pedal extensions help a student in a wheelchair, or one who has other difficulties, reach the pedals of the piano. These devices are often used for young children whose legs are too short to reach the pedals. The Foot Pedal Stool is adjustable to seven positions, from 6 to 10 1/2 inches. If these special devices are not available, ordinary stools can be adjusted to support the feet and assure comfortable seating.

Music Stands

Music stands can be adapted for each individual to bring the music closer; for instance, extensions can be welded to the stands to curve around such instruments as the tuba. For people who have only peripheral vision, a stand can be placed to one side. The American Printing House for the Blind (Louisville, Kentucky) distributes a music rack that fits onto the piano's music rack and can be adjusted to bring the music closer to the player. The Royal Conservatory of Music in Toronto sells a cardboard rack that hangs from the piano music rack. It is not adjustable but it does bring the music closer.

Holders

- Use Plasticine or masking tape to hold drums to tables or to the tray of a wheelchair.
- Make stands of wood with holes drilled through to hold wind instruments such as recorders.
- Neck holders, sold for instruments such as the guitar, can be adapted to hold light wind instruments.
- Clamps can be attached to xylophones to secure them to tables, desks, chairs, or beds. Velcro can hold down small drums and other small percussion instruments.
- Sew bells onto mitts, socks, leg warmers, hats, etc. so that children with little motor control can move these easily and be part of an ensemble. Bells can also be sewn onto a piece of elastic and slipped over a finger or hand.
- Use velcro straps to hold rattles and shakers in place in hands or on legs or arms.
- Suspend instruments from music stands, snare-drum holders, or wooden stands for ease of playing, particularly for students in wheelchairs.
- Use U-shaped, adjustable hospital tables to make the instruments more accessible.
- A small frame made of wood can have instruments such as woodblocks suspended from it, and can sit easily on a bed.

Picks

Making modifications to picks can sometimes enable a person with poor pincer grasp to strum a guitar, ukulele, or autoharp. Here are some ideas:

- Glue a pick to the finger of a glove using rubber cement.
- Make a sleeve for a finger from stiff plastic and glue a pick to this.
- Cover a tongue depressor with masking tape and use as a strummer. A teething ring also makes a good strummer and is easy to hold.

- Cut a large pick made from a piece of stiff felt. This can be attached to an arm, leg, toe, or headpiece with a Velcro strap. Large, easy-to-hold picks are also sold commercially.
- Spatulas that have rubber ends make good strummers and are easy to grasp.

Mallets

Mallets are difficult to hold because their handles are very small. The following ideas might help:

- Enlarge the stick by wrapping it in carpet tape, pushing the handle through a piece of Styrofoam shaped like an egg or slipping the handle through a piece of rubber hose or even a bicycle handlebar grip and holding it in place with masking tape.
- Using masking tape or Velcro straps, tape a beater to a hand, a foot, or even a headpiece to facilitate playing.
- Make a strap of Velcro or leather to go around the hand and to contain the handle of the mallet.
- Put an elastic around two ends of a mallet and over the back of the hand to hold the mallet securely in place.

XII LEFT AND RIGHT

Many students of all ages (not only those with special problems) confuse left and right. This is one reason why many people have difficulty reading a map. Have the children mark their hands and/or feet so that they can distinguish between left and right more easily. Always mark the same side (always the left or always the right) so the side that is marked is immediately obvious. Here are some other ideas:

- Tie a piece of ribbon or heavy macramé twine around everyone's right hand and right foot.
- Use tiny bells sewn onto an elastic or a ribbon. This is an excellent device for visually impaired students.
- Draw a happy face on the back of one hand.
- Slip a decorated pony-tail elastic in place over one hand.
- Draw an "L" on the back of the left hand and an "R" on the right.

XIII 3/4 AND 6/8 METER

Music in 3/4 and 6/8 meters seems to calm people, especially autistic and emotionally disturbed children. Meters such as 2/4 and 4/4 push the listener from one point to another. These meters move people in space and that is why they are used for stirring marches. Music in 3/4 and 6/8 – such as lullabies, cowboy songs, and sea chanties – tends to stay in one spot and to rock back and forth.

If students come to the music lesson in a disturbed or "hyper" frame of mind, play gentle music in 3/4 or 6/8 meters while they sit or lie on the floor quietly. They can rock gently from side from side while listening. This will produce a calming effect.

Teaching students to play and/or sing music in 6/8 or 3/4 meters will also encourage a fairly relaxed and peaceful atmosphere.

XIV HOLDING HANDS

Young children do not have trouble holding hands with each other in games and dances, but as they grow older holding hands becomes more of a problem. The following activities can be performed by the students to get around this problem:

- Have them do the movements with their hands on their hips.
- The students could hold a small piece of ribbon or a scarf between each person.
- When performing songs that require holding hands (e.g., "Mulberry Bush"), have them stand still, drop hands, and clap the rhythm pattern of the words when singing the last line. This helps to keep them from squeezing each others' hands.

XV PUPPETS, DOLLS, AND STUFFED TOYS

Using puppets with children can stimulate their imagination and creativity. Use puppets to dramatize well-known stories or to create new tales. Puppets are also wonderful for focusing attention.

There are many different kinds of puppets (finger puppets, paper bag puppets, puppets made from gloves, puppets with papier-maché heads, rod puppets, and so on). Children and older students can often make these themselves.

Try teaching a song or clapping rhythms by using a doll, puppet, or stuffed toy. Echo work and rhythm clapping can be more effective if small cymbals are sewn to the hands of the toy. This gives the student something to listen to as well.

Shy or disturbed children will often relate to a puppet or toy when they are too frightened to respond to humans. The child will sing with the puppet, answer questions, and carry on whole conversations with these inanimate and nonthreatening objects.

XVI MUSIC APPRECIATION

> Whether you listen to Mozart or Duke Ellington you can deepen
> your understanding of music only by being a more conscious and
> aware listener – not someone who is just listening but someone
> who is listening FOR something (Aaron Copland, *What to Listen
> For in Music*).

When students undertake the study of singing or playing an instrument, they should also receive a background and appreciation of the
whole tapestry of music – the history, the various styles, the composers, and so on. This information must be appropriate to the student's age and level of understanding.

When students are studying music by a certain composer, the
teacher could lead a discussion of his or her life – its trials and tri-
umphs. The teacher could play other music by this composer as well.

The teacher might wish to undertake a comparison of similar forms
in musical literature. For example, if the music to be learned is a minuet by Haydn, discuss the minuet form (ABA) through the use of
symbols (▲ ● ▲) and/or letters; clap a rhythmic pattern that begins
with a small motif, follows with a different motif, and then repeats
the first part; play minuets by other composers.

Discuss why the tempo of the minuet is fairly slow (e.g., the man-
ners of the times, the restrictive clothing of the aristocracy). Show pictures of people dressed in the finery of the times.

A brief discussion of the society in which the composer lived and
worked will help to place the music in time.

There are many recordings and books (at all levels of understanding) that will prove helpful to the teacher.

This kind of approach not only teaches the student to play an
instrument but also gives an education in music that makes the whole
subject more relevant and interesting.

Older students might wish to delve more deeply into the background of the music and to take courses in music history. These
courses can be adapted to the students' level of understanding. There
is a huge range of recorded material to choose from. Listening to such
recordings as *Beethoven Lives Upstairs*, *Mr. Bach Comes to Call*, *Mozart's
Fantasy*, and *Ring of Mystery* by Suzanne Hammond or *Peter Ustinov
Reads the Orchestra* is an excellent way to teach as well as entertain.
These recordings have become popular with a wide range of students
from the very young up to adults (see Chapter 10 – "Books, Records,
and Tapes").

Focusing on recorded music for more than 20 to 30 seconds at a time can be a real challenge for some students. For people with special needs the difficulty is often compounded. The following ideas might help:

1. *Prepare the students beforehand.* Tell them the story of the music (adapted to their level of understanding) or talk a bit about the animal, person, or place the music describes. Talk about whether the music will be soft or loud, fast or slow, when the trumpet part repeats, and so on.

2. *Play short selections.* If you want to use a longer piece, break it up into several shorter segments.

3. *Play the selection one time, then ask a question:*
    - Is the music fast or slow? Is it loud or soft?
    - Does the music get faster or slower? Louder or softer?
    - Who is singing (man/woman/child/choir)?
    - How many voices/instruments can you hear?
    - How would you draw the sounds?
    - Are there many high notes?

    Play the selection again and see if the answers were correct. Repeat with another question.

4. *Do activities with beat while listening:*
    - Keep the beat with your hands and feet.
    - Walk the beat with your fingers on a lapboard or the tray of a wheelchair.
    - When the music changes, change the place where you were keeping the beat (for instance, tap your knees to begin and change to tapping your shoulders). This will show the form very graphically.
    - Transfer the beat to unpitched instruments such as drums or sticks. (Don't use too many or the result will be a deafening noise.)

5. *Do more difficult activities with rhythm:*
    - Write a rhythm pattern from the piece on the board or on a chart. Everyone claps or taps it. Have the students show in some way when they hear the pattern in the music.
    - Have several people clap different simple rhythmic patterns to accompany a piece of music that has a strong beat.
    - Play these rhythms on unusual percussion instruments such as cowbells, an aufiche (cabasa) or guiro, as well as drums and sticks. Combine as many instruments as the students feel comfortable with and use the patterns to accompany a recorded

selection that has a strong beat such as a march. Some examples follow:

6. *Do activities with melody:*
   ■ Have the students put their hands up when they hear the music go up, and lower them when the music comes down.
   ■ Draw the contours of a melody on a chart and have the students trace them with their fingers as they listen to the music. Use large sheets of paper and large crayons, markers, or paint brushes.
   ■ Draw several melodic contours on a chart, including one that is in the piece of music you are listening to, and have the student pick the correct one.
   ■ Have the students talk about whether the melody goes up, down, or mainly stays on one note. Does it skip around or proceed smoothly by step? Is it smooth or jagged? Does it have large leaps or small ones?
   ■ Can the students match the contour maps with the actual notation?
   ■ Count the number of times the main melody is heard.
   ■ Those who are able to could learn to play the main melody on a keyboard or xylophone.
7. *Do activities with form:*
   ■ Tell students that the first part of a piece (in ternary form) is repeated. Ask them to indicate when they hear the repetition.

- Would the pattern look like ▲ ● ▲ or ▲ ● ● ?
- Play the beat of different sections on different instruments.
- Show the form graphically for younger students and with letters for older ones (▲ ● ▲ or ABA).

8. *Do activities with instruments:*
   - Describe an instrument that will be heard in a selection of music. Show a picture of it (or present the actual instrument) and play a short recording of its sound. Play the selection and have the students indicate in some way when they hear the instrument. A good example would be the clarinet heard in the opening of *Rhapsody in Blue* by Gershwin.
   - Ask the students to name two or more instruments heard in the selection.
   - Give out a list of instruments (or use pictures) and ask the students to circle those heard in the piece.

9. *Do other activities:*
   - Ask the students to name the meter of a piece. Give some preliminary help by clapping and counting the beat in several measures.
   - Without telling them the title of the selection beforehand, ask the students to make up a name for it. What do they think the music is describing?
   - If the selection is typical of the music of a certain country, ask the students to find the place on the map. The music could spark a discussion of the customs, history, and art of that country.
   - Many selections have been the subjects of illustrated books. Use these to stimulate interest – for example, *Tubby the Tuba* by G. Kleinsinger, *The William Tell Overture* by Rossini, *The Nutcracker Suite* by Tchaikovsky.
   - The students could paint pictures about the events in a piece of music. Try works such as *March of the Toys* by Herbert, *Peer Gynt Suite* by Grieg, or *Star Wars* by Williams.
   - Have the students listen first, then move to the music. Try "Waltz of the Doll" from *Coppelia* by Delibes or "The Ballet of the Unhatched Chicks" from *Pictures at an Exhibition* by Mussorgsky.

XVII EXAMINATIONS

Students who have special needs and who wish to take music examinations often need adjustments made for their particular disability.

Most schools and conservatories will agree to these once the problems are pointed out to them.

1. People with visual impairments can be given an extra question in ear training to compensate for not being able to do the sight reading section.
2. Many conservatories (specifically the Royal Conservatory of Music in Toronto) provide large-print examinations and also theory examination questions that have been transcribed into braille. If the student is communicating in braille, a separate room can be provided so that the noise of the brailler will not disturb others.
3. People with hearing difficulties can be given an extra sight reading question to compensate for the ear training section, which they might be unable to do.
4. People with learning disabilities that make reading difficult and others (who are perhaps visually or physically impaired) who find it impossible to write, can be given oral examinations.
5. Extra time can be allowed for those with learning disabilities, visual impairments, and other problems such as arthritis.
6. Adjustments can be made in the examination room for physical disabilities – height of tables, supports for instruments, and so on. Although many public buildings are wheelchair-accessible, this is sometimes not the case. The place where the examination is held may have to be changed to allow access for special candidates.

XVIII RECITALS

Many students who have special problems also suffer from poor self-esteem. The idea of playing in a recital or before any gathering of people can create terror and even cause them to stop taking music lessons altogether. People should never be forced to participate in recitals if they do not want to. There may come a time when they might change their minds about playing in public, but it is best to wait until that time comes and they suggest it.

Some people would be happy to take part in a recital if they could use their sheet music. Having their music in front of them relieves the fear of forgetting the piece and making a mistake.

Sometimes a young child can play for a favorite doll or arrange a group of stuffed animals into an "audience" for a concert that he or she will play. This often makes the student less fearful about playing for a live audience. Again, it should be the student's choice.

2 MENTAL DISABILITIES

●●

PEOPLE who have mental disabilities are often tremendously interested in studying music and taking part in musical activities. They love to sing, play instruments, and dance, and many become quite proficient. Success in these activities develops a sense of self-confidence and accomplishment that often cannot be obtained in any other way.

DESCRIPTION

There are five generally accepted classifications of mental disability, although these "labels" are gradually being abandoned.

Borderline, Intellectually Disabled

- General IQ around 70 to 85.
- Capable of completing up to grade 7, 8, or 9 level of education.
- Need remedial work to succeed but can integrate into society quite well.

Mildly Disabled

- General IQ 50 to 70.
- Can attain around grade 5 or 6.
- Will most likely become a fully-functioning adult, holding down a job that is not too demanding intellectually.

Moderately Disabled

- General IQ 35–40 to 50–55.
- Capable of attaining a school level of approximately grade 2.
- Could become semi-independent but will probably function best in a sheltered workshop/group-home environment.

Severely Disabled

- General IQ 25 to 35–40.
- Are taught basic self-help and language skills. Often these people cannot speak.
- Often have other handicaps.
- Most live in institutions.

Profoundly Disabled

- IQ below 25.
- Often have multiple handicaps.
- Require total nursing care.

These categories are only generalizations. Individuals may perform at higher or lower levels depending on variables such as the presence of other disabilities, background, early upbringing and teaching, emotional stability, and so on. Each person is unique.

The music educator will most often be involved with individuals who fall more or less into the first three divisions, while a music therapist might work with the severely and profoundly disabled.

The causes of mental disabilities can be genetic, but, in the case of a mild disability, environmental conditions often play a part as well. Some of these conditions are poor nutrition on the part of the mother during pregnancy; poor nutrition of the child during his or her earliest years; drug or alcohol abuse by the mother during pregnancy; and neglect of the child leading to an absence of physical and mental stimulation.

Down syndrome (a congenital disorder caused by a chromosomal abnormality) and rubella in the mother during the first three months of pregnancy can cause slight retardation, but most often result in more severe disabilities.

CHARACTERISTICS OF PEOPLE WITH MENTAL DISABILITIES

1. People who have a slight, mild, or moderate disability acquire knowledge in the same order and sequence as other people but at a much slower rate.
2. Because their short-term memories are poor, repetition is important. The material should be presented in many different modalities (visual, auditory, tactile, kinesthetic) so that the information can be absorbed through the person's strongest modality.
3. Language skills are often poor. Find another way, other than just

speaking, to present information – for example, use sign language, pictures, songs. Always work to improve language skills.
4. People with mental disabilities are easily distracted and have difficulty focusing on the work.
5. People with mental disabilities have no hesitation in showing their feelings and saying exactly what they think – good or bad. Often these people have a different sense of space from ours – they come in far too close to others. Children tend to be on top of you all the time, in your lap, and right up under your nose. One of the tasks in dealing with people who have mental disabilities is to teach them to deal with space, and the world in general, in socially acceptable ways.

It is refreshing to work with those who have mental disabilities, but it can often be a little unsettling for teachers who are not prepared beforehand.

MUSICAL "SAVANTS"

One of the most unique groups of people with mental disabilities are the so-called "savants." These individuals have low IQs (sometimes as low as 40 but generally falling into the 60 to 70 range) but exhibit exceptional skill in a particular subject. These subjects include the mechanical memorization of dates, the calculation of complex mathematical equations, as well as art, music, and playing chess.

Those with musical ability may far outstrip the normal population. They can play whole pieces of music after one hearing. Their retention of dates and facts about music is often excellent, but they show no ability in other school subjects and often are unable to cope with everyday life.

Researchers who have studied these musically adept people have come to the conclusion that IQ and skill in music and some other subjects are unrelated and that one can have low general ability and one highly developed skill at the same time.

When musical talent is discovered, every effort should be made to encourage it. Some people have learned to talk through the medium of song. Self-esteem and the joy of producing and appreciating music can be the result of training and support.

Teachers working with musical savants will have to take into consideration their incredibly focused train of thought. The teaching will be mostly by rote as note reading will be far too difficult for most.

TIPS FOR SUCCESS IN MUSIC ACTIVITIES

1. Try to work in an environment free from distractions.
2. Make sure everyone is comfortably seated. Some people need a slight support to sit easily on piano benches, chairs, or floor; many children do not wish to sit on the floor at all. Inexpensive plastic "booster" seats can sometimes be used to solve this problem.
3. Don't talk – do. Concentrate on activities, not on comments and descriptions.
4. Keep the activities simple.
5. The material used must be appropriate to the age of the students. Try to find songs, activities, and music that are not too babyish but are still within the capabilities of the group. Popular songs often have fairly simple melodies and words. Use these with older students.
6. Present materials using a variety of techniques. People learn in different ways. Use a multi-sensory approach – movement, singing, speech patterns, poems, playing instruments (see Chapter 1, Section VI – "Movement").
7. Be concrete. Abstract ideas and modes of presentation are a waste of time. Use pictures, models, Plasticine, wooden "notes," model cars, trucks, houses, puppets, and so on.
8. Repeat, repeat, repeat, but in as many different modes as possible to keep up the interest.
9. Engage students in activities that call for responses, independence of thought, and decision making (e.g., sound exploration projects, singing songs in which the words change, inventing instrumental parts).
10. Plan to cover less material than usual. Break down each task into mini-steps and proceed to teach these steps in sequence. Be sure that one step is mastered before going on to the next. This method is often called "chunking."
11. Note reading should be taught only if the students are capable of learning it. Remember that musical notation is almost completely abstract and it may not be worth taking the time to have the students master it. Teaching the songs and music by rote may be more worthwhile because so much more can be covered and interest can be sustained.

    Some people with mental disabilities can learn to read rhythms by means of pictures, words, rhythmic notation, or a system that depicts the sounds with long and short lines or sticks. These approaches are very concrete.

Melodic notation is very difficult because it is even more abstract than rhythmic notation. If your students can read letters, presenting the song with just the letter names often works well; for example, G A B G G A B G B C D – B C D – and so on (Frère Jacques).

Instead of letter names use colors or picture stickers placed on each note (see Chapter 1, Section VII – "Notation").

SINGING

Singing is an important social activity. It provides an effective emotional outlet, improves speech production, and can be a vehicle for learning. For small children (and others too) almost any type of information can be taught through song, for example, numbers, colors, days of the week, and self-help and safety skills.

For older people with mental disabilities, singing groups can be a great source of joy and a valued social experience. The emphasis here is on participation. However, choirs can be formed that concentrate more on performance and quality of sound. Higher-functioning students with good voices can often participate in a regular choir.

Many students with mental disabilities have voices in the lower ranges. Pitching songs at their level will result in more successful participation. Songs that have easy melodies and deal with interesting subjects are most often the best choices (see also Chapter 1, Section VIII – "Singing").

INSTRUMENTS

People with mental disabilities have historically been able to play almost any instrument successfully. In making a choice, it would seem that some instruments are more appropriate than others. For example, brass and woodwind instruments (especially the clarinet or saxophone), are generally easier to play than strings.

Electric organs that supply the correct chording are popular and useful, since the student has only to play the melody and everything else is provided.

Accordions, melodicas, and unpitched percussion instruments such as drums are good choices, as are all types of melodic percussion instruments (xylophones, metallophones, glockenspiels), whose notes can be removed to suit the abilities of each player.

Whatever the choice of instrument, the student should be able to assemble, disassemble (if necessary), and maintain it.

It will probably be necessary to rewrite parts to suit individual players or to divide one part among several students in an ensemble. Such an ensemble can create a full, musically rich sound to which each person contributes in a small or large way depending on ability.

One of the most successful musical groups for people with mental disabilities is the handbell choir. In these groups, the players follow charts with the individual bell parts written out. Depending on the abilities of the group members, these charts can use numbers, letters, or different colors to indicate when a bell is to be rung. Some groups who are lower functioning use a light board. Each player has two bells, one for each hand. A board with two lights is set up in front of the bells. When the light comes on over a bell, the player rings it. The boards are centrally controlled by the leader. (See *Let Everyone Ring* by Joe Pinson in the Bibiliography to this chapter.)

The keyboard lab is an excellent teaching environment for many special-needs students because it provides a nonthreatening and relaxing atmosphere. Again, each person can be given a part to play that suits his or her needs; the use of earphones focuses each student's attention.

People with mental disabilities, especially those with Down syndrome, sometimes have other problems, including deformities of the hands. Electronic instruments are often more successful for these students than conventional keyboards because they are so much easier to play (see Chapter 1, Section IX – "Instruments" for other ideas).

BIBLIOGRAPHY

Alvin, Juliette. *Music Therapy*. Rev. ed. Auriel Warwick. London: John Clare Books, 1983.

Anesthesia, Anne, and Raymond Levee. "Intellectual Deficit and Musical Talent: A Case Report." *American Journal of Mental Deficiency* 64 (January–February 1960): 695–783.

Bailey, Phillip. *They Can Make Music*. London: Oxford University Press, 1973.

Bergmann, Jerry, and Wallace DePue. "Musical Idiot Savants." *Music Educators Journal* (January 1986): 37–40.

Dervan, Nancy. *Orff Schulwerk for the Mentally Handicapped*. Norwood, MA: The Music Player's Press, 1980.

Dobbs, John P.B. *The Slow Learner and Music*. London: Oxford
    University Press, 1966.
Nordoff, Paul, and Clive Robbins. *Music Therapy in Special Education*
    2d ed. St. Louis, MO: Magnamusic Baton, 1985.
Pinson, Joe. *Let Everyone Ring* (Handbells for Special Populations).
    Sellersville, PA: Schulmerich Carillons Inc., 1990.
Silini, Flora. "A New Dimension in Piano Teaching." *The American
    Music Teacher* (April–May 1983): 28–30. An article on teaching the
    student with a mental disability.
— *Experiencing Music with the Piano* (Teaching Piano to Students Who
    Have Mental Challenges). Video. Available through Very Special
    Arts Productions, Education Office, The John F. Kennedy Center
    for the Performing Arts, Washington, DC, 20566.
Streeter, Elaine. *Making Music with the Young Handicapped Child*.
    London: Music Therapy Publications, 1980.
Viscott, David. "A Musical Idiot Savant." *Psychiatry* 33(4) (1970):
    494–515.
Ward, David. *Hearts, Hands and Voices*. London: Oxford University
    Press, 1976.
— *Sing a Rainbow*. London: Oxford University Press, 1979.
— *Sound Approaches for Sound Learners*. London: Bedford Square Press,
    1971.
Wood, Miriam. *Music for Mentally Handicapped People*. London:
    Souvenir Press, 1979.

For other titles that would be useful in working with mentally disabled people, see Chapter 10 – "Books, Records and Tapes."

3 PHYSICAL DISABILITIES

●●●●●●●●●●●●●●●●●●●●●●●●●●●●●●●●●●●●●●●

DEPENDING on the severity and type of problem, people with physical disabilities can often succeed very well in music. Some have health problems but still have the full use of their limbs; some have crippling conditions that affect their ability to play but still allow them to sing; some have lost the use of their lower limbs but have manual and vocal dexterity. Each person is unique, and different adaptations must be made for each.

DESCRIPTION

Health Problems

For many people a physical disability may take the form of a chronic health problem such as cystic fibrosis, heart trouble, asthma, diabetes, or AIDS. These problems are usually under control medically, and the students are able to pursue normal musical studies. The most urgent problem to guard against is over-exertion, especially in children's music classes that include movement.

Epilepsy

Although epilepsy is a serious health problem, it can be well controlled medically. There are two kinds of epilepsy: grand mal and petit mal. Grand mal leads to seizures that can include falling down, convulsive movements, and loss of consciousness. These seizures occur infrequently; but if one should take place, remain calm, remove anything that can hurt the student and allow the seizure to run its course. With petit mal, the person may blank out for a few seconds, and then take up where he or she left off when the seizure is over. Some people have as many as 100 of these in a day, and this, of course, makes learning very difficult. Information may have to be repeated many times.

Cerebral Palsy
Cerebral palsy is an irreversible, nonprogressive condition caused by damage to the brain at birth. Depending on the area of the brain that is damaged, the person with cerebral palsy has varying degrees of control over trunk, limb, and head movement. Some can walk with crutches, braces, or a cane; others are in wheelchairs.

There are three kinds of cerebral palsy, and some people have a mixture of these.

Spastic
- These make up the largest number of people with cerebral palsy.
- They walk with a scissorlike gait with bent knees, arms held out to the side to assist balance or held close to the body.
- Their hands are often turned toward the chest.

Athetoid
- These people have uncontrollable, jerky movements, which become more pronounced when they try to do such things as play a drum or hold a mallet.
- Their heads are often drawn back and they tend to drool because they cannot control their mouth muscles.

Ataxic
- These people have problems with balance and motor coordination because of damage to the balance center of the brain. Often the result of a car accident.
- There is unsteady movement of the limbs and eyes.
- If these people walk at all, they tend to bring their knees up abnormally high in front of them with each step.

Many people with cerebral palsy require positioning and mobility equipment such as specially built chairs, tricycles, pushers, and wheelchairs. Some may have to use a headpiece to type or play a drum.

Electric wheelchairs that can be controlled by a stick or pressure pads on the chair's tray have given these students a new lease on life. For many it is the first time they have ever moved on their own.*

---

*At the McGee Clinic in Toronto, Dr. Karen Pape has had great success in helping patients become more mobile by electrically stimulating specific muscle groups. The results have been just short of miraculous, as patients have gone from being completely dependent on wheelchairs to walking with crutches or even walking unaided. These results have been well documented with videotapes of each stage.

Because people with cerebral palsy do not have normal muscle control, they are often considered to be retarded. Some are, but many are not. Often there is an exceedingly bright brain trapped in a physically disabled body, unable to communicate thoughts and feelings because the muscles of speech do not function. Teachers should never underestimate the potential of these people.

The challenge is to find alternate means of communication for each person. Several electronic devices have been developed to assist people with motor disabilities. One is an electric scanner that flashes a continuous alphabet and a series of numbers on a screen; the person just hits a button or electric pad to type each letter (or number) as it moves by. This method is slow, but effective.

Blissymbolics is a method of communication developed by Shirley MacNaughton at the Hugh MacMillan Rehabilitation Centre in Toronto. In this method, which is based on the ideas of Charles Bliss, common words, letters, and certain ideas have a symbol. Each child has an individual selection of symbols to which he or she points as needed. Fairly complicated ideas and emotional concepts can be communicated without the need to read print. Blissymbolics is used throughout the world as a means of communication for people with cerebral palsy. Here are a few examples of the symbols used in Blissymbolics:

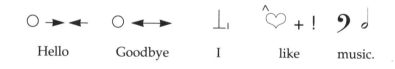

| Hello | Goodbye | I | like | music. |

The drawback of Blissymbolics is that the signs are often based on abstract reasoning concepts. Many people prefer to use a pictograph system, which gives a more concrete symbol for the word or idea.

Muscular Dystrophy

Muscular dystrophy is a hereditary disease characterized by a slow, progressive deterioration of the voluntary limb and trunk muscles. The first symptoms of the disease are frequent falling, difficulty in getting up, and clumsiness in such activities as running, climbing, and catching a ball.

Students with muscular dystrophy require a great deal of emotional support – they know that their condition will only get worse. Music activities can help keep them active with games and movement while providing them with a new interest. Music can also provide a wonderful outlet for emotions and a setting for social interaction.

Spinal Bifida

This condition is caused by a failure of the bones of the spine to grow fully, leaving part of the spinal cord exposed. It results in walking difficulties and, in extreme cases, in complete paralysis of the lower part of the body. The upper part of the body is usually normal, so students with spinal bifida often have the dexterity to play musical instruments.

These students tend to become alienated, particularly as they reach adolescence, and so require a great amount of ego reinforcement.

HOW MUSIC CAN HELP

Music can be a source of comfort and learning for all these students especially as they grow older. Playing an instrument or listening to music will help improve their quality of life. Cassette players and CDs have opened up worlds of music for many people at the push of a button.

Music can also be a source of contact with the outside world. In schools, singing in the choir or playing in groups gives opportunities for social interaction. People with disabilities can make a meaningful contribution in the field of music right through adulthood. Wayne Pronger of Toronto, for instance, has been writing and recording country and western songs for many years despite being severely disabled by cerebral palsy.

Depending on their intelligence, most students with a physical disability can cope with a regular music program, although in some cases instruments may have to be modified (see "Instruments" below). It is important to push these students to their limits so that they will experience the joy of accomplishment.

Listening Appreciation Programs

These programs will facilitate listening with intelligence. All kinds of music, from Palestrina to Madonna, should be included along with music from many lands and cultures. In this way, people's horizons will be expanded. Make sure the students are listening *for* something – for example, where the trumpet enters or how the rhythm first heard in the drum part is repeated in the brass section, and so on. (See also Chapter 1, Section XV – "Music Appreciation.")

Movement

Movement activities help to keep the muscles active and to maintain a general state of health for students with physical disabilities. Do action and game songs that involve movement; carry the children through the actions or push them in wheelchairs if they cannot move in any other way. Volunteers are useful to help in these activities.

Children with physical disabilities have difficulty perceiving how a normal body operates symmetrically. Sing walking songs and have the children sway to the beat or "walk" their fingers on the lapboard. Gently swing small children to the beat in large pieces of strong cloth held securely between two people.

Developing the student's sense of the body in space can be helped by doing movements to recorded music, performing action songs, and playing position games. For example:

I move my hands up, up, up,
I move my hands down, down, down,
I move my hands to the side, and back,
Then I move them round and round and round.

Finger plays will encourage a child to become familiar with that most vital sensory tool – the hand. For example:

Here is the church,
Here is the steeple,
Open the doors
And there are the people.

Movement exercises can help toe walkers (children who walk on their toes because the contraction of their muscles prevents them from placing their feet flat on the floor), especially those suffering from muscular dystrophy, to walk normally and can delay the inevitable shortening of the Achilles tendon.

Caution: Never pick up a child or move a limb without a thorough knowledge of that child's condition. Doing so may injure the child. Be aware that they cannot help you move them because of their condition. They may also have the added poundage of braces. It is also very easy to injure one's own back if care is not taken.

Wheelchair Dancing

There is a growing interest in wheelchair dancing worldwide. In Great Britain, as many as 100 people of all ages have taken part in countrywide wheelchair dance festivals. In these festivals activities are organized for a variety of participants: those in electric wheelchairs, those who can operate their chairs manually, and those who can push only with their feet. Traditional folk dances, modern dances, and dances created by the contestants are some of the events.

TIPS FOR SUCCESS IN MUSIC ACTIVITIES

1. Use masking tape and Velcro straps to attach drums and other small instruments to trays and tables, and to secure mallets and small instruments to hands and feet.
2. To help students keep the beat, have them move scarves or pieces of crepe paper knotted together. This adds interest and gives force to the movement.
3. Use Nerf balls (made of foam) or yarn balls for throwing and catching. They are easier to grasp and will not hurt if someone misses.
4. Attach such items as balloons, scarves, or small instruments to wheelchairs for easy retrieval.
5. Put paper under each student's hand or use a little liquid soap in a flat pan to let them swish their hands back and forth in time to the music.
6. Have several activities that will be easy for those who cannot speak, for example, creating sound effects with mouth sounds, playing instrumental accompaniments, and so on.

SINGING

People confined to wheelchairs or those who use crutches tend to hunch over and slump in the middle. This diminishes their lung capacity and the result is very shallow breathing. Singing can be a great help in overcoming this problem because taking deep breaths to sing develops the lungs.

1. Have the students reach up and follow the upward contour of the melody. If they cannot move their arms, ask them to reach up with their chins, the top of the head, the nose, the chest!
2. Attach a balloon with a long string to a wheelchair and have the students try to keep it up in the air by tapping it.
3. Practice good breathing techniques.

Most people love to sing, given a little encouragement, and people with physical disabilities are no exception. Some have extraordinarily beautiful voices. There are many choirs and singing groups made up of people with physical disabilities.

Often a person's disability affects the organs of singing, and accuracy of pitch is not possible. This in no way should lessen the joy that they can feel when singing. "Babbling" songs or speech patterns can be created for those who cannot talk; older students can try the scat-singing syllables if they have difficulty with real words (see Chapter 1, Section VIII – "Singing").

INSTRUMENTS

Percussion

Drums and small unpitched percussion instruments are suitable for students with physical disabilities. These instruments are easy to grasp and can also be attached to a hand or foot with Velcro or elastic.

Make drums from long pieces of plastic sewer pipe cut to the correct length so that one end can rest on the floor and the drum head on the other end can reach the level of a bed or wheelchair. Top the drum with a plastic or skin head held in place with steel circular clamps.

Whole conversations can be created using only drums. (This can be a good activity for nonverbal students.) Drum playing can also be a good medium for working out aggressions, especially, again, for nonverbal students.

Orff Instruments

Xylophones and other "Orff" instruments are tremendously adaptable for playing by physically disabled students. Take off all the notes that are not needed – whatever the player hits will still sound correct. These instruments fit nicely on wheelchair trays or even on beds.

Autoharps, Guitars, and Ukuleles

Autoharps, guitars, and ukuleles are popular choices for students who have some manual dexterity. There might have to be some modification in picks or tuning to make playing them easier (see Chapter 1, Section XI – "Modifications for Instruments, Beaters, and Picks").

Keyboards

Pianos might be possible for some students, but electronic keyboards offer more exciting possibilities for the majority. These instruments take little strength to play and can even be activated by fingers that curl under or are otherwise deformed. Some keyboards automatically produce rhythm and/or chords to accompany the student's melody. Combining several keyboards and a drum machine will give a satisfying, "grown-up" sound. The student can play the melody on one keyboard while the teacher (or another student) plays the accompanying part. Sometimes special braces can be made to support the student's hand and wrist and enable him or her to extend the fingers into a playing position.

Recorders and Orchestral Instruments

Recorders and orchestral instruments can be played by people who have some physical disabilities. Stands might have to be made to help the student hold the instruments. There is even a one-handed recorder in existence!

Students with deformed fingers might better choose an instrument such as a mellophone or horn whose keys are flat and easier to press than those on, say, a trumpet. Violins and other stringed instruments would be very difficult for these students.

Strings

Instruments such as violins, violas, cellos, and guitars can be restrung backwards to allow a person who does not have good use of the fingers in the left hand, but whose right hand is normal, to finger the notes with the right hand. Holders and other devices can be used to help the student grasp the bow with the problem hand. Artificial hands can hold a bow.

See Chapter 1, sections IX, X, and XI, for a fuller discussion of instruments and adaptations.

Developing a good self-image is very important for students with physical problems, especially as they grow older and become more aware of their disabilities.

Music activities can give all students a chance to accomplish something meaningful on their own and can also be a source of comfort and an outlet for emotions.

There is nothing quite as wonderful as the feeling of intense joy that comes from participating in music. Physical challenges should not be allowed to prevent anyone from experiencing this joy.

BIBLIOGRAPHY

Clarke, Cynthia, and Donna Chadwick. *Clinically Adapted Instruments for the Multiply Handicapped.* St. Louis, MO: Magnamusic Baton, 1985.

Elliott, Barbara. *Guide to the Selection of Musical Instruments with Respect to Physical Ability and Disability.* St. Louis, MO: Magnamusic Baton, 1983.

Herman, Fran, and James Smith. *Accentuate the Positive.* Toronto, ON: Jimani Publications, 1988.

Hobson, Neil, arr. *Piano Music for One Hand.* Disabled Living Foundation, Music Advisory Service. National Music and Disability Information Service, Dartington College for the Arts, Totnes, Devon, England.

Krout, Robert. *Teaching Basic Guitar Skills for Special Learners.* St. Louis, MO: Magnamusic Baton, 1983.

Shawcross, Frank. *Nine Carols for Christmas.* Disabled Living Foundation, Music Advisory Service. National Music and Disability Information Service, Dartington College for the Arts, Totnes, Devon, England.

The Spastics Society. *Wheelchair Dances*, Books 1–3.

United Cerebral Palsy Association. *Cerebral Palsy: What You Should Know About It.* (Available from United C-P Association Inc., New York, NY, USA.)

See Chapter 10 – "Books, Records, and Tapes" for a selection of general-interest books that would be suitable for use with people with physical disabilities. See Chapter 11 – "Useful Addresses" for information on obtaining materials.

4 VISUAL DISABILITIES

●●●●●●●●●●●●●●●●●●●●●●●●●●●●●●●●●●●●●

FOR people who are blind or partially sighted, music can be one of their most valuable experiences, bringing them joy and comfort. Music can also contribute to the development of auditory and social skills, and (when combined with movement) can help overcome a lack of spatial awareness and poor mobility skills.

Many blind musicians, like José Feliciano, Ray Charles, and Stevie Wonder, have achieved extraordinary success in the field of music. Most people, however, will study music to enrich their own lives and to create a bridge to the sighted world.

Although people with visual impairments are no more musical than the general population, they have been trained to develop their auditory sense from their earliest years and may grasp musical concepts more easily. If they have attended a residential school for the blind and visually impaired, they will probably have been exposed to many more musical experiences than their sighted peers. Musical training is an important part of the curriculum for most of these schools. It is an interesting fact that about 12 percent of the students attending residential schools seem to have perfect pitch, contrasted with about one person in a thousand in the general population.

DESCRIPTION

The following are general descriptions of visual impairments. Different countries and jurisdictions often include additional criteria such as the condition of the field of vision.

1. *Normal vision* is described as 20/20 – a person is able to read the "20" line on an eye chart from a distance of 20 feet.
2. *Partially sighted* people have 20/70 to 20/200 vision. They see objects at 20 feet that normally sighted people can see at 70 to 200 feet. The test is taken with the better eye and with correction, that is, glasses.
3. *Legally blind* people have 20/200 vision or less, with correction in the better eye.

DEGREES OF BLINDNESS

1. *Guiding vision* – ability to perceive forms well enough to move around.
2. *Perception of form and motion* – ability to see within a range of two to four feet.
3. *Light perception* – ability to distinguish night and day.
4. *Totally blind* – no light perception whatever.

OTHER VISION PROBLEMS

1. *Peripheral vision only* – in which a person can see only out of the outer edges of the eye.
2. *Tunnel vision* – in which a person has only a narrow field of vision straight ahead.
3. *Distorted vision* – caused by astigmatism, an irregularity in the curve of the cornea. The light rays coming to the eye do not converge to a focal point.
4. *Albinism* – a condition characterized by a lack of the pigment that filters out light rays. Some people with albinism are literally "blinded" by the sun.
5. *Cataracts* – a clouding-over of the fluid in the lenses. This condition appears most often in older people; however, congenital cataract is also an infant eye disorder. Surgery can often correct the problem.

CAUSES OF BLINDNESS

Historically, the most common causes of congenital blindness were an excess of oxygen given to premature children in incubators (retinopathy of prematurity) and the onset of rubella in the mother in the first three months of pregnancy. Improved medical care has reduced the incidence of retinopathy in premature infants. In Western nations, rubella has been all but eliminated by vaccination.

The most common causes of blindness today include diabetes, accidents, cancerous tumors behind the eye (retinoblastoma), inflammation of the cornea, and glaucoma.

HOW MUSIC CAN HELP

Development of Spatial Awareness

Fear of space is an understandable result of poor vision. It hurts to fall. It hurts to crack your leg on an unseen table. It hurts to trip over a curb. To develop spatial concepts, mobility training should be a large part of the education of people with visual impairments.

1. Perform songs and activities to develop body awareness and spatial relationships. Have older students participate in a variety of dances, from square dancing to disco.
2. Pair a student with visual impairments with a sighted "buddy" for movement activities.
3. In dances use the circle formation first (to give a sense of security) before going on to lines or squares.
4. Be careful of asking blind children to hold hands with others. Their hands are their eyes and their means of defense. Restraining both hands may lead to terror.

See Chapter 1, Section VI – "Movement" for other ideas.

Cognitive Development

All of us – especially young children – absorb a great amount of knowledge and general information (about 80 percent) through our eyes. People with visual impairments are not able to do this. Although the blind and partially sighted have the same wide range of abilities and intellectual capacities as their sighted peers, they must work much harder to keep up. Almost everything must be memorized. Braille reading is, at best, only one-third to one-half as fast as normal reading. Thus, for the visually impaired student, the auditory sense is vitally important for learning.

For young children, much language can be acquired through song. There are songs about almost everything – numbers, colors, days of the week, months of the year, and so on. Older students can learn songs and music of different countries and historical periods and through these songs learn about history, geography, and various social customs.

Emotional and Social Development

The frustration felt by people with visual impairments is often expressed in anger. This fact, plus the inability to detect nonverbal communication – a smile or a frown – can lead to failure in social situations.

1. Music is effective because it is a very social activity – it can help people with visual impairments relate in positive ways to others.
2. Music (especially music in 3/4 or 6/8 time) can relax and calm people.

3. Playing instruments (particularly drums) can give a safe outlet to express feelings such as anger and frustration. Singing is also a marvellous outlet for emotions.

4. An ability to play an instrument or to sing well can be a bridge to the sighted world.

5. By providing a constructive activity, music can help eliminate the so-called "blind mannerisms" that some people have, including rocking in space, eye poking, head bobbing, and so on.

TIPS FOR SUCCESS IN MUSIC ACTIVITIES

1. Take the student(s) on a tour of the music room before the first lesson, familiarizing them with the location of chairs, tables, electronic equipment, instruments, doors, windows. If you change the arrangement, be sure to let the student(s) know.

2. Use raised line figures and boards to give tactile clues. Even though advanced students will study braille music, they should have a knowledge of standard music notation.

3. Make staves, notes, sharps, and flats from twine glued to cardboard or from sandpaper.

4. Cut two pieces of metal screen the desired size, place them together, tape the sharp edges, and place a piece of paper on top. Write or draw on this with a soft pencil. The resulting lines can be easily felt by the fingertips. This is faster than using glue or twine and can be used to teach theory and other subjects as well.

5. Label everything with braille for the older students: flash cards, xylophones, Autoharps, individual notes.

6. Record material on cassettes for students to use for individual study. Play orchestral and choir parts on tape. This saves hours of classroom time.

7. If sighted and visually impaired students are in the same group, always remember to read out loud what you have put on the chalkboard or are showing from a book.

8. If a visually impaired person has some sight – for example, an ability to perceive light and darkness – visual distractions may make it difficult for him or her to attend to auditory stimuli. Have a source of light that is constant, not flickering.

9. When presenting a sound-maker or instrument for the first time, let the student examine it at his or her own speed using all the senses: touching it, smelling it, listening to the various sounds it can make.

10. Do not have too many background sounds while working with

students who are blind. It makes it harder for them to attend to a specific task or sound. It is not a good idea to have background music playing when they are performing a different task.

11. Talk to blind people as you approach them. Call them by name, say who you are, and tell them what you are going to do. This is especially important if you are moving a person from one place to another.

LEARNING MUSIC

There is no one method for teaching music to the visually impaired. The following approaches can be used in different combinations. Since all the methods depend on memorization, the facts and ideas will be acquired at a much slower rate.

Rote

The rote method works best in the beginning. The teacher sings, plays, and claps, and the students echo. An important aspect of musical education for visually impaired students involves learning by ear from records, tapes, and the radio, and from other people's playing and singing.

Tapes and Records

Cassette tapes are becoming the preferred mode of learning for the visually impaired. Complete courses of instruction for piano, organ, and guitar are now available on tape, as are lectures on various kinds of music – jazz, opera, classical, folk, symphonies – and even master-classes with famous musicians. See Chapter 10 – "Books, Records, and Tapes" for some suggestions.

Teachers of the blind and visually impaired can record individual parts, solos, or instructions for the student to refer to later. More and more blind students, particularly in university, are taping lectures instead of using braille.

When recording music for students, play each part slowly and separately at first. For subsequent recordings, increase the tempo and add more parts until a finished performance is reached. When teaching keyboard instruments, record the part for each hand separately, then both parts together.

Large-Print Scores

There is a good selection of music available in large-print form for partially sighted individuals. This includes piano scores, song selections (classical, religious, popular), as well as music for organ, strings, brass and woodwind instruments, recorders, and guitars.

Large-print size looks like this:

Einstein, Alfred
MOZART. Oxford University Press, 1945.

The following is an example of a large-print music score:

Braille

Braille is an important means of reading for some blind people. It was invented in Paris in 1829 by Louis Braille (who was himself blind) and consists of a series of raised dots on special paper that are "read" by the fingers. It is not possible to read braille at the speed of ordinary reading even when a person becomes fluent.

There are six dots in the braille "cell," numbered 1 to 6. Each letter of the alphabet has a different combination of dots:

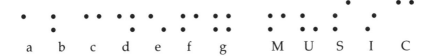

Numbers use the same six-sided cell and are indicated by the placement of the dots 3, 4, 5, and 6 before the letter sign.

Music can also be transcribed into braille. Music braille is very complicated to read, but if students are to become musically independent, they must learn it.

Music braille uses the same cell as letters and numbers, but it is not related. The C major scale reads D, E, F, G, H, I, J in the literary code. This came about because the scale was devised in France where the common name for C is *do*.

The pitch names are shown in the four upper dots, while the time values are indicated by the two lower dots. Pitches are designated by the octave position as well as by letter name.

There are separate signs for sharps, flats, expression signs, and so on, just to complicate matters.

Here is an example of how a bar of music looks in braille:

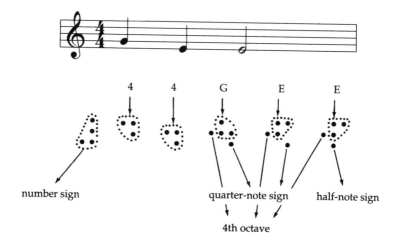

What a sighted person can read at a glance has to be laboriously felt out bar by bar and line by line and memorized by the blind musician. The scores are also very bulky, especially those for piano and organ. Vocal scores or scores for violin, woodwind, or brass instruments are easier to read because they have just one part. A very few orchestral scores have been transcribed for the serious student to read. Beethoven's *Fifth Symphony* runs to six hundred pages!

Schools for the blind usually begin training with an abbreviated form of music braille that leaves out extraneous expression signs. These are taught verbally once the piece is learned.

Brailling is a very expensive and slow process, usually done by trained volunteers. The Canadian National Institute for the Blind

(CNIB) has a large library of brailled music (the second largest in the world, with 18,000 scores) and can often arrange to get special music brailled.

There is also a large selection of brailled music, magazines, and periodicals available from the U.S. Library of Congress, the American Printing House for the Blind, and the Royal National Institute for the Blind in Great Britain. (See Chapter 11 – "Useful Addresses" for more information.)

In addition to learning braille, the student should have familiarity with regular music notation in order to understand references to terms such as "treble clef" or "staff." The teacher might "draw" the staff, sharps and flats, clef signs, notes, and so on, with white glue on a piece of cardboard, by writing on a sheet of paper spread over a screen or by gluing string to cardboard in the correct shapes. These all make the information accessible by touch.

MUSIC APPRECIATION

Students with visual disabilities should be exposed to as wide a range of music and be given as great an understanding of that music as possible. Music can fill many leisure hours with listening pleasure. With the advent of cassettes and CDs, music is now easily available to all. Many public libraries have records and tapes for loan, and courses in music appreciation are available on tape.

SINGING

Most people love to sing, and visually impaired people are no exception. When choosing songs for young people, keep the following points in mind:

1. The songs should have a movement component (for mobility practice).
2. The songs should be about something the students know or some subject that fascinates them, e.g., dinosaurs.
3. Choose songs that develop basic knowledge (days of the week, colors, numbers).
4. Select songs that have a limited range – no great leaps or tricky rhythms.

Older students can be taught good vocal production and can form singing groups or choirs. Some can be integrated into a sighted choir. The music can be transcribed into braille for the student to read (although because of its great bulk, some means of holding it will have to be devised). In a mixed group (sighted and visually impaired), a buddy system can be set up to help the singer with the conductor's cues, signals to stand up or sit down, and so on. (See Chapter 1, Section VIII – "Singing" for further suggestions.)

INSTRUMENTS

Playing an instrument can be a source of delight and satisfaction for people with visual impairments. Their involvement can range from creating a song accompaniment on a drum to playing in a band or full orchestra.

Drums and Other Small Percussion Instruments

These instruments are easily held and played and can be used to hold a small "conversation" between two people. Rhythm patterns can be worked out on unpitched percussion instruments before being transferred to other instruments such as the piano or clarinet. The student can create accompaniments to songs, or play rondos, rhythmic canons, and so on.

Orff-like Percussion Instruments

Xylophones, metallophones, and glockenspiels are excellent for beginners since notes may be removed, leaving only the notes the student will need. This will ensure success. Individual tone bars are also recommended since the child is responsible for only one note. Later, as skill develops, the student will work with a full keyboard.

Pianos, Electric Keyboards, Organs, Recorders

People with visual impairments have enjoyed great success learning these instruments. Attention must be given to exercises for "feeling" one's way around the keyboard.

Band and Orchestral Instruments

When choosing any instrument, especially a band or orchestral instrument, allow the students to explore it tactilely at first. As a matter of fact, the students should be exposed to all the orchestral instruments in this way so they will have an idea of what they are like. Experiment with playing the instrument, putting it together, and taking it apart. Each student must be able to do this without assistance.

1. All instruments are possible, although it might be wise to avoid double-reed instruments because it will be difficult for students with visual disabilities to prepare their own reeds. For single-reed instruments, use a plastic reed at the beginning, experimental stages.
2. Many students with limited vision have had success playing the violin and other stringed instruments, but these require more individual teaching, especially for the different positions and proper bowing.
3. Brailling the parts will be necessary for blind students. Some students playing with a group will be expected to read as they play. Sometimes this requires the construction of a special device to hold the instrument, thus freeing one hand to read the braille. For some instruments this will be impossible, and the student will be expected to memorize the part before rehearsal.
4. Students who read large print must have stands adapted and raised so the music can be held two to three inches from the eyes and the instrument held underneath.

   Some lyres (such as the long trumpet lyres, which have the music holder attached to a long stem) can be extended so that they wrap around the instrument to bring the print very close. Be careful to keep the music in front of the student so that he or she is able to see it while keeping the instrument in the proper playing position.
5. Playing position and posture must be taught verbally, by setting the person's hands correctly on the instrument or by having the student "see" with his or her hands exactly what you are describing.
6. Embouchure is especially difficult. The student might be helped by the following verbal images:*
   - Tonguing – Tell the student to think of a ball of paper on the tip of the tongue, peashooter style.
   - Lip position – Suggest that the student draw or pull the wet, fleshy part of the lip against the teeth to imitate braces.
   - Cheek puffing – Suggest that the corners of the lips stick to the surface of the teeth.

Handbells and Chimes

Most of the music for handbells and chimes will be learned by rote, but some teachers have created their own music brailling system to

*I am indebted to Bill Murphy and the Music Department of the Ross MacDonald School for the Visually Impaired in Brantford, Ontario, for the following ideas and also for some of the above suggestions.

allow the students to read their parts.
See Chapter 1, Section IX – "Instruments" for further suggestions.

BIBLIOGRAPHY

Burrows, Anne. *Music through Braille*. Edmonton, AB: M.E. MacNab Publishers, 1987.

Davison, June, and Ardella Schaub. *Piano Progress: An Approach to Music for the Partially Sighted*. Pittsburgh, PA: Volkwein Bros., 1972.

Dykma, Dorothy. *They Shall Have Music. A Manual for the Instruction of Visually Handicapped Students in the Playing of Keyboard Instruments*. Carbondale, IL: 1986.

Hoffer, Don. *Guitar School for the Blind*. A comprehensive course on tape to teach guitar to the visually impaired.

Homespun Tapes. Woodstock, NY. This company offers both video and audio tapes to teach an amazing variety of instruments, from bluegrass guitar to keyboards. Vocal instruction on tape is also available.)

Jenkins, Edward. *Braille Music Primer*. Louisville, KY: American Printing House for the Blind.

Krolick, Bettye. *Dictionary of Braille Music Signs*. Washington, DC: Library Service for the Blind and Physically Handicapped, Library of Congress.

Levinson, Sandra, and Kenneth Bruscia. *A Curriculum for Teaching Optacon Music Reading*. Layfette Hill, PA: Tembrook Press, 1983.

Pederson, Gale. *Key to the Keys* and *Easiest Way to Improvise*. Tulsa, OK: Piano Playhouse, 1971, revised 1990. Audiotapes for learning to play the piano. These have been very successful in teaching visually impaired students.

See Chapter 11 – "Useful Addresses" for information on how to obtain the materials and books mentioned above.

5 HEARING DISABILITIES

DEAFNESS, often called the hidden disability, can be even more debilitating than more obvious impairments. People who cannot hear are cut off from normal communication. Even people who have a slight hearing loss feel out of place in large groups. Because the ability to hear is fundamental to developing language for the young child, deafness also impedes the acquisition of knowledge.

DESCRIPTION

There are two categories of hearing impairments, based on the severity and nature of hearing loss.

The Hard of Hearing

- Involves mild to moderate loss of hearing. Speech can be understood with hearing aids.
- Students with this degree of hearing loss can often cope in regular schools, but they need extra help in developing language and usually have a hearing specialist visit them regularly.

The So-Called Deaf

- Marked by severe or extreme loss of hearing, although most possess some residual hearing.
- Students are usually trained in special programs at schools for the deaf.
- Children must be taught from infancy to use what residual hearing they have and (depending on the program) are also taught sign language, lipreading, and/or finger-spelling as aids to communication.

Some students in this second category are congenitally deaf. Some have become deaf after birth (adventitiously deaf). Those who become deaf after birth have an advantage in terms of speech acquisition because the rhythms and inflections of speech are present in the brain and can be utilized as a basis for speech training.

TYPES OF HEARING LOSS

Conductive Loss

- Usually results from problems with the middle ear and can sometimes be corrected by an implant operation.
- There is a fairly uniform loss across all frequencies, low to high. Amplification by means of a hearing aid will improve the ability to hear all frequencies equally.

Sensorineural Hearing Loss

- Caused by damage to the inner ear (i.e., the tiny hairs of the cochlea) and/or the auditory nerve.
- Damage usually results in the loss of the upper frequencies (above 500 cycles per second, or middle C in music), although there are a few people who have the capacity to hear only extremely high sounds such as dog whistles. At present there is no way to correct sensorineural damage.
- Ordinary hearing aids are not very successful with this type of hearing loss because they cannot sufficiently amplify the problem frequencies. However, hearing aids can sometimes amplify sounds enough to give cues that would help understanding. For instance, if a person says "Shut the door," a deaf person might not be able to hear the exact words, but might pick up the underlying rhythms of the sentence. This is often an important clue for understanding the meaning.

Some people have both conductive and sensorineural hearing loss.

HOW SOUND IS MEASURED

Sound can be described in terms of frequency and intensity. Frequency is the number of vibrations produced per second and is measured in hertz (Hz). Intensity refers to the loudness of the sound and is measured in decibels (dB).

Frequency

Humans are capable of hearing sounds between 20 and 20,000 Hz. The most important frequencies for understanding speech are between 500 Hz (middle C) and 2,000 Hz (the C two octaves above middle C). This is the range in which nerve loss is most pronounced; so you can understand the disastrous effect it can have on speech. Much music also lies within this range.

Intensity

A special scale has been created to describe intensity by means of a unit called a decibel (dB). An intensity of 0 dB is equal to the quietest audible (QA) sound (e.g., leaves rustling) and every 10 dB is equal to ten times the previous sound energy. The following table compares the intensity of familiar sounds.

Breathing	10 dB	$10 \times QA$
Whispering	30 dB	$1,000 \times QA$
Normal conversation	50 dB	$100,000 \times QA$
Vacuum cleaner	70 dB	$10,000,000 \times QA$
Snowmobile	90 dB	$1,000,000,000 \times QA$
Chainsaw	110 dB	$100,000,000,000 \times QA$
Jet engine	120 dB	$1,000,000,000,000 \times QA$

It is becoming increasingly common in our society for people to suffer hearing loss from prolonged exposure to loud noises – jet engines, chainsaws, tractors, pneumatic drills, factory noise, and very loud rock music. These noises all exceed the threshold level at which hearing loss can occur (80–90 dB). Listening to Walkman radios and cassettes with the sound turned up too high is another common source of hearing damage. Many players in rock bands have experienced partial hearing loss and have taken to wearing ear plugs when they play and avoid standing in front of their loudspeakers. Players in symphony orchestras are also vulnerable, since they are exposed to sounds between 85 and 90 dB for hours each week while practicing and giving concerts.

LEVELS OF HEARING LOSS

People who have hearing impairments are described by the degree to which ordinary speech has to be amplified in order to be perceived (see table following). Severely or profoundly hearing impaired people may not be able to distinguish speech sounds that are over 500 to 1,000 Hz even with amplification of 80 to 90 dB.

Mild (slight)	20–40 dB
Moderate (mild)	41–55 dB
Marked (moderately severe)	56–70 dB
Severe (severe)	71–90 dB
Profound (extreme)	91 dB and above

CAUSES OF HEARING IMPAIRMENTS

Prenatal

- Hereditary – 50 percent of all deafness is hereditary.
- The mother had rubella in the third month of pregnancy when the auditory processes were being formed.
- Prematurity or Rh blood factor incompatibility. Rh-positive and Rh-negative blood are not compatible. During second or subsequent pregnancies, a mother who has Rh-negative blood will produce antibodies that attack the red blood cells of the Rh-positive fetus, often causing deafness.

Postnatal

- Meningitis and measles, with their extremely high fevers.

HEARING AIDS

Hearing aids have improved greatly over the past few years due mainly to the development of the transistor. Unfortunately, no hearing aid is perfect. Hearing aids pick up everything – classroom sounds, traffic noises, and noise from radiators and air conditioners.

If you teach students who wear hearing aids, try to keep the music room as quiet as possible and refrain from playing the drums and cymbals too loudly, since these sounds might be amplified over the students' pain threshold.

HOW MUSIC CAN HELP

Many adults who have a hearing loss have expressed their frustration in not being encouraged to pursue music studies as a child. The desire to participate in music activities seems to be a universal trait even within the deaf community. All people want to create music and experience the joy and sense of satisfaction that making music can bring.

For people with hearing impairments, music can help in many ways, for example:

1. *Music can encourage relaxation* for those who are frustrated at not being able to hear and communicate through speech. Activities such as shaking out individual body parts to a drumbeat, performing dances to songs and instrumental selections, and combining breathing with movement, will help keep the student relaxed. A relaxed body will, in turn, foster learning of musical ideas.
2. *Music can help develop listening skills.* Young children need to develop the ability to focus on one sound – i.e., speech – to the exclusion of background noise and other extraneous sounds. Sound location games played with kazoos, drums, horns, and/or whistles sounded out of sight of the students are good activities. So too are echo clapping, sequencing sounds, and recognizing and moving to walking, running, galloping, and skipping rhythms played on drums. These rhythms can be represented graphically or by notation (if the students can handle this) and then played by the students themselves on unpitched percussion instruments.
3. *Music and movement activities can foster good posture and a graceful way of walking and moving.* This helps to build self-confidence.
4. *Music can encourage language acquisition.* By singing the lyrics to songs and saying poetry out loud, the student can practice the inflections and rhythms of speech.

TIPS FOR SUCCESS IN MUSIC ACTIVITIES

The Hard of Hearing

Although many of the activities suggested for people who are deaf are also useful for working with the hard of hearing, there are certain differences, so I will discuss them separately.

Students who have a hearing impairment are usually strong in the visual, kinesthetic, and tactile modes of learning. Their weakest areas are in verbal communication, social development, and general knowledge (much of what we know of the world comes to us almost subliminally through our ears).

Students who are hard of hearing can usually take part in a regular music program, although their ability to sing in tune may not be well developed.

1. When teaching music to hard-of-hearing students, try to build their confidence by emphasizing their strengths, then work to develop the weaker areas.
2. Present information in as many different modalities as possible.

3. Be sure hearing aids are working properly.
4. Face the students when giving verbal instructions. They need to be able to see your lips.
5. Use many visual clues – pictures, flashcards, models.
6. Sing some songs in a lower key than usual. People who are hard of hearing will be able to understand them better.
7. Clap and walk the beat and rhythms, and play these on percussion instruments. Make them visual. This approach uses many modalities of learning.
8. Use classroom instruments. This gives opportunities for success in ways other than singing.
9. Teach songs that have actions and dances and encourage creative movement.
10. Teach songs the students might encounter in everyday life so that they will be able to participate with others.
11. Encourage hard-of-hearing students to play the piano or an electronic organ or synthesizer where the sound can be fed back through earphones. Clarinets and saxophones are also good because the vibration of the reeds can be felt (see "Instruments" below).

The Severely and Profoundly Hearing Impaired

Young students with a severe and profound hearing loss are most often sent to special schools. Formerly these schools were residential but now facilities are being set up to teach these students in their own school boards.

Each student must be assessed carefully, and many factors should be taken into account before a teaching method is decided on. Some of these factors are: the intelligence and motivation of the person, the degree and kind of deafness, and the dedication and commitment of the parents to reinforce language and music skills at home. This is true in the private music setting as well as in school.

Students who are severely and profoundly hard of hearing have such great difficulties learning that they are often three to four years behind in school. Music teaching will have to be taken at a slower pace. Since lack of language is the main drawback, every teacher, no matter what subject, must become a teacher of language as well.

There are different methods of teaching people who are severely and profoundly hearing impaired. No one way is best. A combination of techniques (total communication) is the most effective method for most students:

1. *The aural/oral approach* trains the residual hearing of the child through amplification of sound. This method is very slow and difficult to teach. However, in Holland, Denmark, and parts of England, the use of music with this method has had dramatic results in helping children learn the inflections and rhythms of speech.
2. *Sign language* offers an instant form of communication. Its advocates say that it leads to earlier comprehension of words and hence better reading skills. It also reduces the frustration of not being able to communicate verbally and is the preferred means of communication in the deaf community.
3. *Speech reading (lipreading)* should be combined with other methods since 40 to 60 percent of speech sounds cannot be seen.
4. *Finger spelling* is helpful as a supplement to sign language when there is no sign for a particular word.

General Tips

1. Sing songs in lower registers. Anything over C above middle C becomes difficult to detect.
2. When playing recordings, choose those sung by men or by women with low voices. Raffi and Hap Palmer are good suggestions for children because the tempo of their songs is slower as well.
3. Sit on a level with the students' faces to make it easier for them to see your lips. Do not cover your lips with your hand while talking. It is difficult to lipread men who have beards or moustaches.
4. Speak distinctly, in a moderate tempo – not too fast but not so slow that the speech rhythm is distorted.
5. Use concrete aids such as pictures, models, puppets, and so on. Hold them up near your mouth so that the students can lipread at the same time as they are looking at the object.
6. Try to work in a place that has a wooden floor, or have a platform constructed so the students can feel the vibrations through it. Placing speakers face down on the floor will intensify the sound.
7. Place two or three speakers in a long, benchlike case and have the students sit on this while music is being played.
8. Have older students learn social dances, square dances, and other popular dances. The decibel level of most popular music is usually around 100 to 110. It might be best to turn off any hearing aids so that the sound does not go over the pain threshold (120 to 130 dB).
9. Signed songs are helpful. On the following page is an example of a song in American sign language. Be aware that signs differ from country to country and even within communities in these countries.

Are You Sleeping?
(Frère Jacques)

  Palm up. Hand moves down *or* point to someone.

 Hand over face fingers spread out – moves down. Fingers come together.

 Palm in little finger up, others curled under thumb. Twist out to right, slightly downward motion.

Are   **you**   **sleep-**   **-ing**

 Hand at temple moves down – two index fingers together

 Make a "J".

Brother   **John?**

 Left hand on right arm at elbow. Right hand extended palm up, moves upward (sun rising).

 Right hand, closed fist hits palm of left, then shakes out to right.

"R" sign moves out from in front of lips.

 Right hand, fingers extended, shake away from left palm.

Morning   **bells**   **are**   **ringing**

 "D" sign hits palm of left hand.

 "D" sign (with right hand) hits left palm, then shakes away as in "ringing".

ding   **ding**   **dong**

It is important to decide on signs that give a sense of the words but also keep time to the music and allow the flow of the singing to move gracefully. Words such as *the*, *an*, *and*, and *a*, and endings such as *-es* and *-ing* are often left out so that the important words can be signed exactly on the beat.

Signing choirs, which integrate hearing and deaf students are very successful. One of these, in Rockville, Maryland, has the wonderful name "Fabulous Flying Fingers."

10. With older students, make charts of the words of the songs and poems. Say the words, clap the rhythm patterns, and play these on a drum. Have the students sign the words while you point to them on the chart. This will give them added practice in reading and will keep up the flow and tempo.

11. The music teacher may find it advisable to learn some words and phrases in sign language or to create some of his or her own especially for musical terminology. Sign language suffers from not having specific signs for rests, quarter notes, and so on. A special committee of concerned teachers of the deaf is now trying to compile an acceptable sign vocabulary for these terms and to get it adopted by the signing community.

MOVEMENT

People who are severely to profoundly hearing impaired often lack movement skills. Movement, speech, and rhythm are so interrelated that severe hearing loss (which produces a stilted, unrhythmic speech) can result in an uncoordinated, shuffling kind of movement.

The deaf cannot hear people coming from behind and this often results in a fear of space and a hunched-over kind of walk. A good movement program combined with music can help alleviate these problems. Moving to drumbeats, performing set actions and dances to songs, creating movements to describe a story or song, dancing to rock and roll, performing folk dances from countries throughout the world – all these activities will assist deaf people in overcoming their fear of space and help them to move with ease and grace. (See Chapter 1, Section VI – "Movement" for more ideas.)

SINGING

Many of the sounds produced by people with hearing impairments will not be very musical, but in spite of that, try to encourage singing.

Singing helps develop breath control, speech, and language. Songs can be found on almost any topic (numbers, colors, days of the week) and can fit in with other school subjects very well. Signing songs while singing helps communication and can be very graceful to watch. Try to play songs on the bass keys of the piano or organ or on bass xylophones. The low notes produce easily felt vibrations. Electronic keyboards equipped with earphones are very effective. The students pick up the sound directly in their ears.

INSTRUMENTS

Students with a hearing impairment can successfully play unpitched percussion instruments, especially those that are hand-held and allow the vibrations to be felt immediately.

The vibrations from pitched percussion instruments are also quite easily felt. Students can learn to perceive the low notes (bass xylophones, tympani, bass metallophones) in the legs and lower trunk, the medium tones (alto xylophones and metallophones) in the chest cavities, and the upper notes (glockenspiel) in the head cavities. These instruments can be combined for ensemble playing.

It might be best to pick traditional instruments that have a fixed pitch such as the piano, the organ, electronic instruments, guitar (tune electronically), clarinet, or saxophone. String and brass instruments require a good "ear" and relative sense of pitch. Instruments that produce strong vibrations, such as the clarinet, saxophone, drums, or marimba, are good suggestions.

Sometimes the sense of relative pitch can be transmitted by the student feeling the vibration of the notes on the instrument. For instance, on the trumpet the low B flat, first space F, third line B flat, or fourth line D are all produced by depressing the first valve. The resultant note depends on the speed with which the note is blown and on the embouchure. For a hearing student it is easy to know when the wrong note is played, but a student with hearing disabilities will have to rely on the feel of the vibrations on the bell of the instrument.

There have been many instances of students with moderate to profound hearing loss studying orchestral and band instruments and being integrated into hearing groups. They seem to be able to feel the vibrations of the group as a whole to keep in time and can follow the bandleader's directions easily. (See Chapter 1, sections IX, X, and XI for further ideas.)

BIBLIOGRAPHY

Bang, Claus. "A World of Sound and Music." A paper given at the Conference on Sound Perception, March 8, 1980, at the Oxford Polytechnic, Headington, Oxford, U.K.

Birkenshaw, Lois. "Consider the Lowly Kazoo." *The Volta Review* 77 (1975): 440–44.

— "Teaching Music to Deaf Children." *The Volta Review* 67 (1967): 352–58.

— "A Suggested Program for Using Music in Teaching Deaf Children." In *Proceedings of the International Conference on Oral Education of the Deaf.* Vol. 2. (Northampton, NY, 1967): 1233–44.

Jeff Bradetich. *Broadway for All to Hear* and *Christmas for All to Hear.* Evanston, IL: Easy Hearing Music Inc. These and other titles have been specially produced for the hard of hearing.

Lane, Leonard. *The Gallaudet Survival Guide to Signing.* Washington, DC: Gallaudet University Press, 1978. A handy book of the basic signs.

Music and the Hearing Impaired – Resources for Educators. Compiled by Diane Merchant. Washington, DC: Gallaudet University, 1989.

Proceedings from The Second National Conference on Music and the Hearing Impaired. Edited by Alice-Ann Darrow. Washington, DC: Gallaudet University, 1989.

Robbins, Carol, and Clive Robbins. *Music for the Hearing Impaired and Other Special Groups.* St. Louis, MO: Magnamusic Baton, 1980.

Sacks, Oliver. *Seeing Voices.* Toronto, ON: Stoddart (University of California Press), 1989.

Signed Songbooks

Gadling, Donna et al. *Lift Up Your Hands* Vol I and Vol. II. Washington, DC: The National Grange, 1980.

Wojcio, Michael. *Music in Motion.* Los Alamitos, CA: Modern Signs Press Inc., 1983.

6 LEARNING DISABILITIES

PEOPLE who have learning disabilities do not fit into neat categories. Their disabilities are not primarily due to mental retardation, visual or hearing impairments, emotional problems, or cultural deprivation, although one or more of these problems may be a factor.

People with learning disabilities process information differently from others. They have a jagged learning profile – for example, they may have poor reading skills but excellent musical or artistic abilities; someone who is poor in mathematics may excel at auto mechanics or photography. In contrast, people with mental disabilities have a generally low-potential learning ability in all subjects.

Some people with learning disabilities are extremely bright, but because they have great difficulty in learning to read, they may be labeled as stupid. Often these people find other ways to perceive the world and succeed in spite of their disabilities. Albert Einstein, Nelson Rockefeller, Leonardo da Vinci, and Thomas Edison are four examples.

Learning disabilities in children are often not apparent until the child goes to school and tries to learn to read and write. Problems may show up earlier in delayed speech or an inability to count or to process certain musical concepts.

CAUSES OF LEARNING DISABILITIES

The causes of learning disabilities are not clear in all cases, but certain factors are suspected, including brain damage before or at birth, tumors in the language perception area of the brain, chemical imbalance, inadequate nutrition in the prenatal months or in early childhood, brain injury from car accidents, high fever, physical abuse, a stroke, lead poisoning (from car exhausts or old paint), mercury poisoning in drinking water, or genetic causes.

Some experts believe that learning disabilities may be related to problems in the way the cerebellar-vestibular (the cerebellum and the inner ear) systems process what people see and/or hear.

Several terms have been used to refer to various learning disorders: minimal brain dysfunction, brain damage, communication disability, dyslexia (a disturbance in the ability to read), aphasia, and perceptual handicap. Whatever the cause and whatever the term used, the person with a learning disability requires an individual program of study, tailored to his or her needs.

BRAIN RESEARCH

Brain research is still in its infancy and new discoveries are being made every month. Therefore, it is difficult to describe exactly how the brain works. According to recent research, the brain is divided into two hemispheres, which process different types of information in different ways, but which work together. The two hemispheres are joined by the corpus callosum.

Logical thinking, and mathematics and language processing are believed to occur mainly in the left side of the brain, while global thinking, spatial reasoning, imagery, and the perception of form and pattern take place in the right side.

In terms of music, the left side of the brain is believed to process rhythm and speech (lyrics), while the right side deals with melody. Music appears to be processed more globally than other information. Humming is a right-brain function, while singing words to music is a function of both sides. Playing music by ear is probably more right-sided, while reading music from a score involves the left side of the brain. If the elements of dance and movement (right-sided) are added to the music program, the music curriculum can truly be said to be teaching the whole brain. This makes music a valuable tool for working with students who have learning disabilities – it can sometimes convey information to parts of the brain inaccessible in other ways.

Some researchers believe that when someone listens to music purely for enjoyment, the right side of the brain is involved in the processing. When the person attempts to analyze the music, the processing transfers to the left side of the brain.

Some experts have stated that people with learning disabilities have a larger than normal right hemisphere and that this side of the brain has taken over the functions of the left side (which should be the more dominant). In these cases, the right side tries to process the logical, cognitive activities of reading, writing, and understanding number facts with information gathered in an intuitive, global, nonlinear way.

CHARACTERISTICS OF PEOPLE WITH LEARNING DISABILITIES AND HOW MUSIC CAN HELP

We all learn in different ways, usually favoring one mode of learning over others. Some learn best through the auditory mode, some the visual, and others the kinesthetic. It is important for the teacher to present materials to students in as many ways and modes as possible.

An active music program incorporating melody, rhythm, speech, visual aids, instruments, sound exploration, movement, and dance offers many different ways of presenting the same materials. In such a program, the chances of each person succeeding at learning are far higher than if just one mode were used. The most effective learning technique for most people is a hands-on and participatory approach.

Try to discover what the strengths and preferred modes of learning are for each person and work on those strengths. This will build the student's self-confidence and will serve as a basis from which she or he can tackle the weak areas.

The following is a description of the most common behavioral characteristics of people who have learning disabilities, along with some ideas for using music as remediation.

Inability to Focus on a Task

These students cannot attend to the matter at hand for more than a few seconds. Here are a few tips for getting their attention:

1. Use props – large dolls, puppets, pictures, instruments of all kinds – and change these props often.
2. Drums work like magic. Playing several notes on a metallophone also works well.
3. Sing commands such as "Come and make a circle" or "Put your fingers on the keys." Children attend to sung commands much more readily than to spoken commands. Use as few as two or three notes if necessary.

Lack of Coordination and Poor Motor Skills

Many learning-disabled students have a very poor sense of self in relation to the world around them. They have poor laterality, directionality, body image, and spatial relationship skills and may appear clumsy and uncoordinated. These skills must be improved to increase the students' sense of self-worth and to help them feel accepted. Many researchers believe that if a person does not feel at home in his or her own body, minimal learning will take place and perceptual and reasoning abilities will not develop well.

1. Singing action songs such as "Clap Clap Clap Your Hands," "Bow, Bow, Bow Belinda," or "She'll Be Coming 'Round the Mountain" gives opportunities for developing coordination.
2. Work out rhythms and meters in movement before transferring these to an instrument.
3. Playing these rhythms on a hand-held percussion instrument before transferring them to a piano or violin will help the students assimilate them. Playing rhythms and accompaniments on Orff melodic instruments (xylophones, metallophones) will help develop bilateral coordination and fine motor skills necessary to play a piano or organ.
4. Teach dances to develop coordination.

Communication Difficulties

These are usually the result of not being able to process information clearly and they become apparent when a child does not talk or appears not to understand what he or she hears. Some do not seem to make connections in what they hear; some are able to understand and process the information but cannot express what they feel. Some have varying degrees of all these conditions.

It is important to begin as soon as possible working with children who have these difficulties. Children's songs and nursery rhymes are perfect material as they have constructions and language of the most basic kind – from the child's own world.

1. Sing songs with language that is at the child's level. Songs that have animal, car, or clock sounds to imitate are good – "Old MacDonald," "My Grandfather's Clock."
2. Sing songs in which the words must be changed (by the students) to make a new verse, e.g., "I Love the Mountains," "Aiken Drum."
3. Sing songs with actions.
4. Sing songs about the world to build vocabulary and increase learning.
5. Do sound exploration activities to develop listening skills and encourage the students to talk about what they are hearing.
6. If the students are being taught sign language (some students with learning disabilities are taught this as a primary means of communication), sing songs and use the signs.

Inability to Name Objects

Some children find it difficult to relate an object to its name or symbol. Abstract systems such as letters or numbers become meaningless and reading is impossible. When presented with two slightly different pictures of the same object (a drum for instance), these children will think they are different objects.

1. Try to give sound clues. Play the rhythm of the name of an object on an instrument and have the students say and clap the word back. Relating rhythms to word patterns works well.
2. Present tactile clues – use raised letters, raised pictures of the object, or models made of Plasticine. Try sandpaper cutouts.

Other Perceptual Disorders

- Mirror reading – seeing "p" for "q," "was" for "saw," or ♭ for ♩ and ♩ ♫ for ♫ ♩.
- Wandering letters – the letters do not seem to stay put on the page. One time the students might see "music" but another time see "msuci." The same rhythm pattern could be ♩ ♫ ♫ ♩ one day and ♫ ♫ ♩ ♩ the next.
- Poor short-term and long-term memories. Students sometimes retain information longer when it is introduced in the form of music.
- Inability to sequence. Sequencing is an essential skill in learning. Echo activities of all kinds can help develop this skill, as can singing sequencing songs such as "There's a Hole in the Bottom of the Sea" or "The Green Grass Grows All Around." Present pictures of the items to be sequenced as you sing the song, and have the students put these in order.

Rigidity in Behavior Patterns

People with learning disabilities, children especially, experience such inner chaos that they look for order in their everyday world. Things have to be done precisely the same way every time. Routines for getting up, going to bed, eating, and so on have to be followed exactly. If altered, the results in children are temper tantrums, crying, and general loss of control.

1. Music supplies this order just by its general structure. People have described how music "lifted the perpetual fog" they lived in. "I heard music and the world became clear." Vivaldi, Mozart, Bach, and other composers who wrote very structured music are often their favorite composers.
2. Begin and end the lesson exactly on time.
3. Begin and end the music period with the same song, chant, or greeting.

4. Stick to the same general format for each lesson.
5. Work with repetitive rhythm patterns. Make up rhythms using babbling voice sounds to help speech:

Baa Baa Ba Ba Baa | | ⊓ |

Clap short, repeating accompaniments to songs and poems, then play these on instruments.
6. Children with learning disabilities will often rock, wiggle, or sway to impose order on themselves. Incorporate this motion into the activity. For example, have them rock to the beat of the music.

Hyperactivity

For teachers and families this can be one of the most tiring characteristics of people with learning disabilities. Hyperactive children are always in motion – all day long. Older students sometimes tend to fidget and wiggle and demand new stimulation all the time.

Music can have a calming effect. Often music is the only thing these students will sit still for.

Use music in 3/4 or 6/8 time. This music stays in one place and rocks back and forth. Music in 2/4 and 4/4 time pushes on. It walks or marches from point A to point B and thus forces the listener to go with it. (Each person will react differently, so it is wise to experiment.)

Figure/Ground Perception Problems

People who have these problems are easily distracted, touching and tasting everything they can reach. If they appear not to be paying attention, it may be that they are paying too much attention. It is as if they are unable to separate the important from the unimportant. We all take in thousands of impressions a minute through all our senses, and the task of the brain is to screen out the trivial and allow us to concentrate on the important things. People with figure/ground perception problems cannot do this. Everything becomes important, and they suffer from overload.

1. Work in a calm, distraction-free environment.
2. Keep the music simple – too many parts or instruments will distract.
3. Keep visual material very simple. Do not use music books that have colorful illustrations on the same page as the music. They will just distract.
4. Be aware when listening to orchestral music that the learning disabled might hear an obscure tympani part instead of the main violin theme you asked them to concentrate on.

Emotional Instability

Students with learning disabilities often have extreme reactions to things. This can be a result of frustration in the learning situation, and the response may be wildly disproportionate to the event.

A calm, structured environment and clear signals as to what to do, when to play, and when to stop will head off most of this behavior. (See below for ideas regarding effective lesson planning.)

NOTATION

Traditional notation may be totally baffling to some people with learning disabilities, since it is one of the most abstract forms of communication. Trying to teach it to them may be a complete waste of time.

Try using iconic representations for rhythms and teach melodies by rote. Teaching music through taped lessons and instruments and choral parts can sometimes be successful. See Chapter 1, Section VII – "Notation" for a more in-depth discussion of notation. See also Chapter 10 – "Books, Records, and Tapes" for a list of relevant tapes.

TIPS FOR SUCCESS IN MUSIC ACTIVITIES

1. Always be calm and patient. Never raise your voice or lose your temper.
2. Be sure that you remain in control – be pleasant but firm.
3. Plan, plan, plan. Know exactly what you intend to do and have a backup plan in case of emergency.
4. Never take any props or instruments into the room that you will not use. If they are there, the students will insist on using them. Hide props and instruments until the very moment you are going to use them.
5. Begin and end the lesson exactly on time.
6. Begin and end with the same songs, chants, greetings, or activities and have the same structure for all your lessons. Vary the content but not the structure.
7. Have the lessons in the same place. There should not be too much space that might cause hyperactive behavior. Do not change the appearance of the room too drastically between lessons. Keep the decor simple.
8. Vary the activities between moving and sitting and do not stay too long on any one topic or activity.
9. Be aware that it takes longer for some people with learning disabilities to respond. Give them time.

10. Speak in clear, short sentences. Do not string a lot of commands together such as, "Mike, after you have had your milk, go over to the table and bring me the triangle, the beater, and the drum, and put them on the floor beside my chair." Mike will suffer from overload immediately.
11. Do not ask the students to do too many things at one time – e.g., clap and sing; sing and play a drum; sing, walk the beat, and clap the rhythm of the words. Try having one part of the class perform one action while the rest perform the second action, or just simplify everything the students are required to do. Instruments such as the piano and the organ, which require several actions to be carried on at one time, might not be the best choice for a person with a learning disability.
12. At first, choose activities in which success can be achieved with a minimum of effort. These students can become frustrated and may give up easily. Succeeding in a task immediately encourages them to persevere.
13. Do not try to do too much. People with learning disabilities tire easily because they are trying so hard to learn.

See Chapter 1, sections V, VIII, and IX for suggestions about relaxation, singing, and instruments.

Music is a great socializing force. The joy of making music with others and succeeding at it is a wonderful boost to the morale and self-esteem for students with learning disabilities. Music is often the first subject in which they have ever achieved success.

BIBLIOGRAPHY

Campbell, Dorothy Drysdale. "One Out of Twenty: The Learning Disabled." *Music Educators Journal* (April 1972): 22–23.

Clarke, Louise. *Can't Read, Can't Write, Can't Talk Too Good Either.* Harmondsworth: Penguin Books, 1973.

Clarkson, Ginger. *Moon Sense.* St. Louis, MO: MMB Music Inc., 1990. A play written especially for children who have special needs.

Giacobbe, George A. "Rhythm Builds Order in Brain Damaged Children." *Music Educators Journal* (April 1972): 24–27.

Golick, Margaret. *She Thought I Was Dumb but I Told Her That I Had a Learning Disability.* CBC Learning Systems, Box 500, Station A, Toronto, Ontario, Canada M5W 1E6.

Other resources for teaching students with learning disabilities include Gale Pederson's audiotapes for teaching piano to students with visual impairments; the audio and video tapes available from Homespun Productions; and Mel Bay Publications, which teach a wide variety of instruments as well as voice at all levels. Using a variety of teaching modes might just be the key to successful learning. See Chapter 10 – "Helpful Books, Records, and Tapes" for additional titles. See especially the references to the work of Sheila Mofson, Corrine Roth Smith, and Steven Brown for ideas about different approaches to learning notation and playing the piano.

7 AUTISM

••••••••••••••••••••••••••••••••••••••

A UTISM is a rare and puzzling disorder that affects two to five children in 10,000. There are many adults with autism because in many cases children do not grow out of it. Autism has so intrigued educators, scientists, and physicians that it has produced a great deal of research into its causes and treatments.

DESCRIPTION OF AUTISM

Autism is often confused with childhood schizophrenia, which it resembles. However, for a child to be considered truly autistic, the following conditions must be present:

1. *Early onset of the behavior* – in most cases by three years of age.
2. *Presence of severe language dysfunction.* Autistic children do not seem to be able to use language for communication. It was once thought that they did not use language to develop inner thought processes either, but now with greater insight into the world of autistic people, we know that this may not be true. In many cases, comprehensive language is present and fully developed. Many have even taught themselves to read. Problems arise when they attempt to communicate through language. Sometimes speech will take the form of echoing previously heard words and sentences. Communication may often take the form of screams and grunts.
3. *Poorly developed social skills.* Previously, it was also assumed that children with autism had no interest in people, and indeed they seemed to form relationships with tables and chairs and other inanimate objects rather than with people. With increased insight, many researchers (and parents) now conclude that the desire for normal relationships is present but the body in some way does not respond to let the person demonstrate his or her need for contact. This may be because of an extreme sensitivity to touch that results in a kind of brain overload.

4. *The presence of stereotypical behaviors.* These behaviors might include compulsive rocking, wagging the head, twirling small stones or dry cereal and running these through the fingers, flapping the hands, or clapping. Such behaviors used to be considered a form of self-stimulation but researchers now suspect that they may be yet another manifestation of the lack of control autistic people have over their bodies.

5. *Sensitivity to sound.* Many people with autism seem to have an extreme sensitivity to sound – some just for certain frequencies but others for sounds in general.

6. *An obsessive desire for order.* Many autistic people have this characteristic. Everything must be in exactly the same place. Objects such as dolls, blocks, knives, and forks are arranged in exact order (sometimes the objects are sorted in a system known only to the autistic person). It is thought that this order gives the person a framework that allows him or her to move on to other tasks.

It is difficult to assess the potential of these students because of their severe language and social problems. However, many autistic students have high IQs and, if they can be reached, can often perform well academically.

CAUSES AND TREATMENT OF AUTISM

No one really knows for sure what causes autism. In the past it was thought to be caused in part by the parents' attitudes and behaviors. It is now believed that genetic or chemical factors may be involved.

It seems that the most effective way to work with these students is to join them in their world in order to establish a basis of trust – show total acceptance of their way of perceiving reality and in their competency. Never assume that there is retardation for, indeed, many autistic people have high intelligence. Many people have reported success using a behavior modification technique. This has to be done almost one-on-one and is very intense. Many people with autism perform well at tasks when the reward is pennies, tokens, Smarties, or some other tangible item that can be counted and sorted.

With the success of facilitated communication in reaching these individuals, many of our ideas and descriptions of autism must be drastically revised. The newer thinking suggests that autism might involve a disturbance in motor initiation and regulation – the body will not respond and do what the brain tells it to. Sometimes the person cannot start the movement; sometimes he or she gets "stuck" halfway through and just freezes; sometimes the movement, once begun, cannot be stopped (perseveration).

The act of touching seems to break through the "stuckness," but be aware that, although many have the desire to be close, they also have an extreme sensitivity to contact. If held or hugged, the act may set up overstimulation in the brain, resulting in tantrum-like behavior. The amount of physical contact will have to be carefully measured.

Two new approaches to helping autistic people have many implications for the music teacher: facilitated communication and sound sensitivity training.

Facilitated Communication

Many autistic people in Canada, the United States, and Australia have been helped by a technique known as facilitated communication. The "facilitator" sits beside the client and supports her or his arm and hand, helping the client to point with one finger (curling the other fingers back out of the way). With this finger the client is encouraged to point to a board with pictures or an alphabet board or to type on a computer keyboard or on a Canon communicator (a small keyboard that types out the message on tape).

The facilitator does not choose the picture, word, or message the client wishes to point to or type but lightly supports the client's hand and arm, providing a little resistance or counterweight to the client's movement. After the action of pointing or typing is completed, the facilitator draws the client's hand away from the keyboard or alphabet board, and the client is ready to type or point again.

After several weeks or months, many people who have never communicated are able to make their wishes and thoughts known. Sometimes the results have been miraculous. Students who were thought to be severely retarded have been found to have been reading since the age of three (having taught themselves) and some have even been composing poetry in which they have expressed their frustration at being autistic. A few sample comments describing what it is like to have autism reveal the inner turmoil of these people:

- "It is excruciatingly lousy."
- "I had no means besides screaming to communicate."
- "I'm trapped in a cage and I want to get out."
- "I care about people."
- "I can't help what my body does, I can't control it."

The light counterweight seems to overcome the body's disconnection with the brain and for the first time allows the expression of feelings and ideas. As yet there does not seem to be any change of other so-called autistic behaviors.

Some autistic people go on to speak, others do not (at least not yet). Speech requires very complicated and well developed motor responses. Pointing is very simple. This seems to be the reason why facilitated communication works when the person is not able to speak.

Why this form of facilitation works at all remains a mystery but a great amount of research is presently trying to find some answers. Facilitated communication is also being used to help people with Rhett syndrome and Down syndrome.

The implications of this technique for learning music are immense. Besides giving a means of communication, supporting/holding the arm or hand might be just the impetus necessary for some people to focus their minds on learning to play an instrument.

Sound Sensitivity Training

Many people who have autism complain of acute sensitivity to sound. Some may have hyperactive hearing across the spectrum, but others may have problems only with certain frequencies. You might see children clap their hands over their ears when they hear certain music. The sound really hurts. These people tend to crave quiet spaces and to retreat from the world when things become noisy.

In Switzerland, Dr. Guy Bérard has had good results with sound sensitivity training. The first step in the treatment is to determine the frequencies that are giving the problem and then to play music (through earphones) in which these sounds have been filtered out or reduced in amplification so they will not be activated. The other frequencies are played loudly to stimulate the cells that control the other frequencies. Hopefully, everything balances out and the person does not have the acute sensitivity any longer. The treatment lasts several hours a day for ten or so days. A clinic in Montreal also uses this rather controversial approach. Most people who have been treated in this technique report improvement.

When teaching music we should always be aware that some students might have this hypersensitivity and should try to adjust our choice of music and/or the volume of the sound to make sure everyone remains comfortable.

HOW MUSIC CAN HELP

Studies show that many autistic students love listening to music and respond well to music activities once the initial shyness and fear is overcome. Because music is nonverbal and nonpersonal, it can be perceived by the children as nonthreatening.

Some people with autism have demonstrated an astonishing ability to play the piano or other instruments by ear and can reproduce melodies and accompaniments after only one hearing. Many have perfect pitch.

Music seems to be effective in the following areas.

Making Contact and Initiating Communication

1. Sometimes singing a command instead of saying it will provide another pathway to the brain and result in an appropriate response.
2. Have a small selection of unpitched instruments and sound-makers available to explore and experiment with freely (too many instruments, however, may result in confusion). Allow the student to choose a sound-maker and to explore it in different ways – touching it, smelling it, or examining its shape. Be aware that the student might become fixated on the instrument and form a relationship with it rather than with the teacher or group. Use facilitated communication techniques by supporting the playing hand. This might help the student respond more efficiently.
3. Sometimes a student will start wandering around. You might have to play something on an instrument to focus attention back to the music activity. The student then might echo your sound. Singing a little "please come here" song will often help.
4. Sometimes autistic people will not play an instrument because they are disturbed by the sound. Try playing very softly. Change the instrument to one with a softer tone or one with a different range of frequencies.
5. Later, when the student is playing an instrument, imitate him or her on another similar instrument. In this way, the leader becomes the follower, showing perfect acceptance of the student's efforts.
6. Much later, try to get the student to echo you. At this stage, it is best to restrict the activity to vocal responses or unpitched percussion instruments.
7. Create a dialogue on two hand drums – a drum conversation without words. This can also be done with two people on either side of one large drum.
8. If instrument playing is not possible, communicating through movement might be feasible. Imitate the movements the students

are making at first (spinning, rocking, jumping), then have them imitate yours. A "dialogue without words" can be worked out through movement only.

9. When students are perseverating (e.g., tapping incessantly with hands of feet), play a drum, imitating their beat or rhythm, and then change the rhythm to help them break out of the repetitive activity and move on to the next task.

Developing Speech and Language

Once trust has been established, sing songs that are fun and interesting and that also build vocabulary.

1. Sing songs that require a sound response such as "Old MacDonald" (animal sounds), "The Bus" (sounds of the windshield washer, horn, brakes), or "Dinah" (sounds of instruments).

2. Use songs in which the student sings one word. Pause while the student sings the word – "I'm Gonna Sing" ("When the spirit says sing ... I'm going to clap when the spirit says clap ..."), "Old Woman" ("Are you fond of washing ... of ironing ... of cooking ...?"). For the music to these songs and many others like them, see *Come On Everybody, Let's Sing; Music for Fun, Music for Learning;* and other songbooks.

3. Sing songs that change whole phrases ("Aiken Drum," "Down By the Bay").

4. Take nonsense syllables and put them into speech rhythms. Say these babbling exercises together. This recreates the babbling stage of the infant learning to talk. For example:

5. If the student is repeating a certain phrase over and over, make a meaningful chant out of it; for example, "I'm hot":

I'm hot, I'm hot,
I'm very hot I say.
I'm hot, I'm hot,
I'm very hot today.

Say this, clap the rhythm, and play on an instrument.
6. Use other word patterns and say, clap, walk, and play the rhythms on instruments.
7. Work with simple chants, poems, and nursery rhymes in the same way as above. All of these have pronounced rhythms and simple words. For a more contemporary approach, try some of the shorter chants and poems from Dennis Lee's books (see Chapter 10 – "Books, Records, and Tapes").

Some autistic children have been known to communicate by using little songs or snatches of songs to stand for actual words. One child, for example, hummed "Baa Baa Black Sheep" every time she wanted to go in the car. The family had taken a ride to a farm not long before, and they had sung this song at the time. She associated the song with the car ever after. Needless to say, it took a lot of detective work to figure out the connections, but it was worth the effort to see the child communicating in her own way.

Encouraging Social Interaction

1. Try songs that lend themselves to group participation and social interaction ("Paw Paw Patch," "Bow, Bow, Bow Belinda," "Four in a Boat," for example). Often the act of combining singing with movement will enable the person with autism to engage in movement activities.
2. Use several instruments in the accompaniments to songs so that two or more students can play together. You might have to put the instruments in various corners of the room at first, gradually moving them closer and closer together – a little each day until finally a group is formed as the students lose their fear of being together. The Orff instruments and unpitched percussion instruments are excellent choices for this activity.
3. Action songs and songs with movements and dances are good for helping groups of people interact. They also help develop co-ordination and motor sensory skills.
4. Be aware that because of their sensitivity to touch, people with autism may not want to hold hands.

Instilling Basic Concepts

Autistic students can learn basic concepts, such as numbers, colors, and days of the week, through song. The music and rhythm can be another means of relaying the information to the brain.

Creating Order

1. Many people with autism have a compulsion for order in their lives. Schedules must be adhered to rigidly; knives and forks must be placed just so; coats must be hung up in exactly the same place. Music proceeds in an orderly, logical way and fills the need for logic and continuity in people's lives. Music by Mozart and Vivaldi is particularly effective.
2. Make the lesson plan very predictable day after day. Begin with the same song or activity each time, always review familiar material and end with the same ending song or activity. It is also good to keep the surroundings exactly the same for each lesson. These environmental cues give security and allow the individual with autism to focus and move on to the next task.

Expressing Emotions

1. Many people with autism seem locked within themselves and unable to express emotions. Music listening activities can provide safe outlets for the expression of emotions. Anger can be expressed on a drum. Song lyrics such as "If you're happy and you know it clap your hands" can be changed to "If you're sad and you know it cry a tear" or "If you're angry and you know it stamp your feet." Show pictures of people expressing these emotions or, even better, see if you can photograph the students themselves expressing the emotion and use these for reinforcement.
2. The person might follow up this activity by expressing her or his feelings verbally or through facilitated communication.

INSTRUMENTS

Some people with autism can play instruments effortlessly by ear. For others, teaching them to play will require special techniques.

Once again, facilitated communication would seem to offer another tool to the music teacher. Supporting the hand and applying light resistance might help the student play notes with one or two fingers. Later, if the support could be reduced to supporting the elbow or touching the shoulder, the student may be able to play normally.

Learning by rote is probably the best approach. The teacher can record passages on cassette tapes for the student to take home to practice. For note reading, it is best to start in a very simple way and proceed slowly, adding new material very carefully. The students will need to be drilled on which direction the notes are moving, which ones are on lines, which in spaces, and so on. Always do some activities that involve rote work so the student will have successful experiences in the lesson. (See Chapter 1, Section VII – "Notation" for alternative ways of teaching notation.)

Some researchers, like Thomas O'Connell, have found that the main stumbling block to note reading is rhythm, which is basically a left-brain activity. Students with autism can easily reproduce a melody including the rhythm when it occurs within the context of music that has been heard (a right-brain activity). However, understanding the relationship between note values and reproducing this in notation or from the printed page seems to be extremely difficult and requires much work.

Clapping rhythms, saying babbling patterns to them, using the Kodály time names, walking the rhythms, playing them on hand percussion instruments, and so on, helps provide a whole-body understanding of the rhythms. The chances of success are far greater with this sort of preparation.

Many people with autism respond well to the same methods for teaching notation outlined for people with learning disabilities. (See also Chapter 1, Section VII – "Notation" for further ideas.)

If, after many ideas and approaches have been tried, the student can still not master notation, go back to rote learning and playing by ear. After all, Irving Berlin had a very successful career in music even though he was unable to read music. It is possible to provide enjoyment and a love of music and increase repertoire through rote teaching without adding to the frustration and sense of failure of the student who is incapable of learning notation.

When teaching autistic students, vary the approaches to music learning and the materials used. As soon as the students master the pieces they hear (and this will not take long in many cases), they might just reproduce these endlessly and mindlessly, often talking about something that has no relation to the music at the same time they are playing. To keep the students concentrating on the task at hand, change the tempo or the dynamics, or add a second part on another instrument – anything that adds variety. (See Chapter 1, Section X – "Tips For Teaching Instruments" for further ideas.)

BIBLIOGRAPHY

Biklen, Douglas, and Annegret Shubert. "New Words: The Communication of Students With Autism." In *Remedial and Special Education* 12(6) (November/December 1991): 46–57.

Contact. Toronto: TVOntario Publications, 1980. A film showing the program developed by Fern Levitt for working with autistic children.

Crossley, Rosemary, and A. McDonald. *Annie's Coming Out.* New York: Penguin, 1985.

Kaufman, B.N. *Son-Rise.* New York: Harper and Row, 1976. The story of a family's attempts to educate their autistic child by what were then rather unconventional methods.

O'Connell, Thomas S. "The Musical Life of an Autistic Boy." *Journal of Autism and Childhood Schizophrenia* 4(3) (September 1974): 223–29.

Park, C.C. *The Siege: The First Eight Years of an Autistic Child.* Boston, MA: Little, Brown, 1967.

Prime Time. CBS. With Diane Sawyer. Lisa Hasia and Paul Nichols, editors. January 23, 1992. A program showing how facilitated communication has helped several people with severe autism to communicate for the first time.

Stehil, Annabel. *The Sound of a Miracle: A Child's Triumph over Autism.* New York: Doubleday, 1991. The Story of Mrs. Stehil's autistic daughter Georgie Manly and how she was helped by the auditory training methods of Dr. Guy Bérard.

8 BEHAVIORAL DISORDERS

●●●●●●●●●●●●●●●●●●●●●●●●●●●●●●●●●●●●●

PEOPLE with behavioral disorders may externalize their anxiety and rage in destructive, attention-seeking, and generally uncooperative behavior. They may exhibit prolonged, severe, and frequent bursts of aggressive behavior.

Hyperaggressive students seem incapable of settling to a task. They need instant gratification and may throw tantrums when gratification is denied. Anything that requires concentration, organization, and practice is rejected. Thus, even though many of these students are very bright, they fall behind in their accomplishments. This type of behavior may be the result of living in a dysfunctional family or social environment, or it may have a genetic or biological cause (e.g., a chemical imbalance). Watching many movies and TV programs in which problems are solved by aggression and violence is felt by many experts to compound the problem.

Research also tells us that many of these people suffer from some form of learning disability. This may result in extreme frustration in dealing with the tasks of everyday living. Whatever the cause, more socially acceptable ways of dealing with problems must be found.

Other types of individuals internalize their problems and become anxious and withdrawn. They have very poor self-esteem, are hypersensitive, and appear fearful and shy, crying frequently. As children, their behavior is often confused with childhood schizophrenia or autism because they seem incapable of relating to people and sometimes engage in ritualistic mannerisms.

Withdrawn behaviors may be the result of home environment (including physical or sexual abuse) but may also stem from a learning disability or some genetic or biological cause.

TIPS FOR SUCCESS IN MUSIC ACTIVITIES

For people with behavioral disorders, music represents a neutral, nonauthoritative force that allows them to relax and participate without fear. Students who are hyperaggressive will accept the limits imposed by music. Commands such as "You're out," "Time to stop," and "Go to the center and back" that are part of a dance or musical game are not a threat because they are perceived as not coming from a person. Withdrawn people will be encouraged to come out of themselves and work with this nonpersonal medium.

General Tips

1. *Use music as an organizing force.* Music can set up a kind of inner control, which is needed to counteract the inner chaos present in people with behavioral disorders. Music with a clear beat and predictable form is ideal – especially music by Vivaldi and Scarlatti as well as many marches. Try the following activities:

   - Work with the beat – walk it, clap it, play it on instruments.
   - Play percussion instruments to recorded music in a variety of meters – waltzes, marches, polkas, and so on.
   - Play repetitive bordun and ostinato accompaniments to songs and instrumental melodies on xylophones, glockenspiels, and metallophones.

2. *Use music to help develop social skills.* Even people with severe behavioral disorders will be tempted to join a group to sing, play, and/or dance. Doing this will help them relate to the others in the group. In my classes, I have seen children who had not talked in three years say their first words in the safe environment of a music group, but only after they had sat on the edge of the group for many months watching the activities.

3. *Work in a structured environment.*
   - Always begin and end exactly on time.
   - Set limits and remove the student from the activity or suspend the activity for a short time if the limits are broken. Be very clear and consistent about these limits.
   - Keep calm and never lose your temper.
   - Begin and end with the same song or activity and keep the organization of the lesson the same. Use different material, of course, but retain the same general lesson outline.
   - Have clear routines established for taking out and putting away instruments and other material; never deviate from these routines.
   - If the students are sitting on a hard floor, give them pillows or carpet squares to sit on. This gives them the security of a "place" to come back to and establishes a warm, cozy feeling.

4. *Do gross motor activities.* Try to organize the space so that there will be room for movement activities. This allows for a release of energy and develops coordination. Try songs with movements such as "Monkey See, Monkey Do" or "Hokey Pokey." For older students, simple square dances and folk dances are popular as is dancing to rock music.

5. *Use name songs.* This is especially important with children but adults too feel special when their name is sung.

6. *Use songs that require responses.* Songs that require everyone to make up words, whole phrases, movements, or actions, are excellent – e.g., "Down by the Bay" or "When I First Came to This Land."

7. *Use external stimuli.* A large doll or puppet, or toy car or truck are excellent for children. Pictures, posters, or interesting objects such as unusual musical instruments (a mibira, decorated gourd maracas, special drums, or a guiro) will catch the attention of adults and children alike. All these objects serve to draw the person into the activity and focus their attention.

For Hyperaggressive Students

1. When teaching, change the activity often. These students cannot concentrate on one thing for very long. Keep the same concept but change the way it is presented. To avoid boredom, use several ways to teach the material; for example, "Try it again playing softly / loudly / stressing the first note of the measure / as if a dinosaur is growling / as if a kitten is purring."

2. Try to be aware of what sets off hyperaggressive behavior and prevent it by using a different activity. Be aware that the smallest and most insignificant thing can spark an outburst.

3. If the person is having a difficult day it might be best just to have him or her lie or sit in a comfortable position and listen to soothing music. You could do some passive listening exercises by playing the pieces being studied and talking about them.

For Withdrawn Students

Students who have withdrawn from the world like to have the same thing played or sung over and over. They are gradually drawn into the activity as they feel comfortable and secure in the familiarity of the material.

Music in 3/4 and 6/8 meters is particularly soothing for these people and also seems to have a calming effect on the hyperaggressive student.

INSTRUMENTS

If the students can stay with the task, playing an instrument can help develop concentration skills and organized practice habits.

1. Group classes might not be too successful with students who have a behavioral disability. One-on-one teaching is usually best.
2. The information will have to be presented in small units and for short periods of time.
3. Try to use as many modalities as possible – auditory, visual, and kinesthetic. Sometimes contact can only be made in nonverbal ways – perhaps tactile or through playing an instrument such as a drum.
4. Electronic instruments are useful because they satisfy the need for instant gratification.

BIBLIOGRAPHY

Benenzon, R.O. *Music Therapy in Child Psychosis.* Springfield, IL: Charles C. Thomas, 1982. Includes case studies of severely psychotic young patients and the effect that music has had on their lives.

Gfeller, Kate. "Behavior Disorders, Strategies for the Music Teacher." *Music Education Journal* (April 1989): 27–30.

Madsen, Clifford K., R. Douglas Green, and Charles H. Madson, Jr. *Research in Music Education: Modifying Music Behavior in the Classroom.* New York: Teachers College Press, 1975.

Steele, A.L., et al. "The School Support Program: Music Therapy for Adjustment Programs in Elementary Schools." *Journal of Music Therapy* 13(2) (1976): 87–100.

Williams, L.D. "A Band That Exceeds All Expectations." *Music Educators Journal* 71(6): 26–29. Students in special education can learn to play musical instruments with sufficient facility to form bands. Playing in these has been found to enhance their sense of personal achievement.

9 SENIORS

··

R ECENT research into the leisure activities of senior citizens (see Hanser 1990) shows an overwhelming preference for music. It seems likely that with the projected aging of the population over the next few years, the demand for music lessons and music appreciation classes will increase dramatically.

Some senior citizens may be returning to an instrument they played in the past or they might be fulfilling a life-long ambition to learn a new instrument. Some choose to join a choir of like-minded seniors or to take classes in music appreciation to deepen their knowledge of the whole subject of music. Many seniors return to active concert-going.

This chapter discusses two groups of senior citizens: those who are active and well mentally and physically and those who have some mental and/or physical disability. For the former group, a regular music program can be undertaken (with adjustments made for the increased likelihood of tiring and the longer time it will take to build up the muscles needed to play), while, for the latter, adjustments might have to be made to the instruments or in the way the material is presented.

ACTIVE AND WELL SENIORS

The active and well seniors have their choice of singing and/or playing an instrument. The following are a few points to consider.

Singing

If singing is elected, make sure that the student realizes that the voice deteriorates with age, as does control over breathing. While joining a choir or singing group that sings fairly undemanding music might be a source of intense satisfaction, instruction in solo singing might prove frustrating. Producing clear, well-supported, in-tune notes is difficult at the best of times and becomes more so as one grows older.

Also, the singing range tends to become lower with age. Transposing songs into lower keys may be necessary.

Choosing an Instrument

The choice of instrument will depend on the student's reasons for studying music. The student may wish to accompany others, play in an orchestra, play hymns for a church service, join a jazz ensemble, or just play for his or her own amusement. Music taught in groups such as electronic piano laboratories and Yamaha's Keyboard Club or Electone Club is often a popular choice for older adults as the social aspect is stressed along with the musical.

Some instruments, such as the french horn, require much practice, a well developed embouchure, and good breath control to produce a satisfactory tone. The bass viol requires strong muscles to play well. Instruments such as pianos, guitars, ukuleles, and percussion instruments might be a better choice for study since they are easier to play and will provide more immediate gratification. (See also Chapter 1, Section IX – "Instruments.")

Electronic Keyboards and Electric Organs

These are very popular because they require little strength and often have a built-in rhythm accompaniment. Some, such as the Yamaha Electone have a chording function that can produce the correct chords automatically when the notes of the melody are played. These instruments can be a good choice when the older student encounters great difficulty in coordinating the two hands in keyboard playing.

Electronic instruments also have headphones, which allow the student to play and practice without disturbing others – a major consideration if the student lives in a retirement home.

Handbell Choirs

Handbell choirs are very popular with seniors. Each person is responsible for only one or two bells. Quite complicated and beautiful music can be arranged to suit the abilities of individual players. Charts can be made for the players to read.

Approaches and Materials

There are many good adult beginner books available (see Chapter 10 – "Books, Records, and Tapes" for suggestions). In addition, there are many collections of easy-to-play arrangements of familiar songs that would suit this kind of learner.

It might be a good idea to teach a course on improvisation and "playing by ear" so that the students can derive more immediate satisfaction. If keyboard players develop the ability to chord, they can have hours of pleasure playing from "fake" books, which give the melodies and chords. In their later years, when it may become more difficult to read music, these students will still find enjoyment from playing by ear.

If the students are able to learn notation, then, of course, this should be taught because it opens many doors to the existing music literature and fosters independence in the individual (see Chapter 1, Section VII – "Notation").

Older musicians are valued members of instrumental ensembles, jazz groups, and choirs. Many of these informal groups can be found in most communities.

THE PHYSICALLY AND/OR MENTALLY FRAGILE SENIOR

Many senior citizens who have disabilities are still responsive to music, but activities might have to be adapted to their particular needs. This is not always easy in retirement and nursing homes where there is a great variance in age and ability. Once groups have formed, however, they can provide an intensely satisfying experience. For the physically and/or mentally fragile senior, music can enhance the quality of their lives in many ways.

How Music Can Help

1. *Music can foster communication and social contact.*

The act of singing well-known songs together, doing movement activities (even in wheelchairs), and playing instruments in small "orchestras" enables people to relate to each other without using words. For those who are senile or whose speech has been affected by strokes, this means of communication is vitally important.

2. *Emotions can be expressed through music.*

Music activities offer a place for the safe expression of emotions. Singing songs or playing music that was popular in their youth sometimes allows people to release feelings that have been repressed for many years. Being able to express rage and sorrow about a present or past situation can be a great relief. Music teachers are usually not trained to be therapists and should not attempt to act as one – this is a job for the psychiatrist or psychologist. However, sometimes it helps just to lend a sympathetic ear.

3. Music activities can relieve depression.

Music can become a very important part of the day's program for seniors. It is something to look forward to and something that fills their leisure hours with meaning. The choice of music is important here. Try upbeat, lively selections or slow waltz music with its relaxing and calming effect, and try to assess the effect the selections have on the person.

4. Music activities help to organize time.

Music activities that are programmed into each day can motivate seniors to organize their time better and perform chores they consider unpleasant (see Hanser 1990). "First we wash the dishes and make the bed, then put on that tape of fiddle music you like." By including this kind of organization in their lives, it has been found that many seniors are able to take care of themselves and live on their own for a longer time.

Upbeat, peppy music can help get people going in the morning, while calm, soothing music can help them get a good night's sleep.

5. Music activities encourage exercise.

Moving to music can give pleasant opportunities for exercise. If the people you work with are mobile, then walking and dancing to the music is possible. If they are confined to wheelchairs, they can move their limbs in time to the music (in front, above the head, from side to side), shifting from side to side in the chair and "marching" on the floor from a sitting position. All are very beneficial to preserve suppleness and muscle strength.

Sometimes large balls, scarves, or balloons can be used as aids to movement to add interest and give incentives. Have them hold the balls in two hands above the head, then move them from side to side; hold them out in front of the body and move them from side to side and/or up and down; make large circles with the balls still held in two hands. Scarves can be waved above the head, in front, to the side, in circles, squares, and so on. All of this can be done to music in varying tempi. (See the Bibliography for the names of books that describe these kinds of activities.)

Deep breathing exercises (and singing) will help maintain good breath control and healthy lungs; for example: "Take a deep breath and breathe out for as long as you see my flashlight shine/for as long as it takes to make a large circle in the air with your hands."

Adapting Instruments

Instruments can be adapted to allow for disabilities the students may have so that they can know the joy that comes from making music with someone else.

Many homes for the elderly have "rhythm band" groups. With a little care in the choice of material and some imaginative arrangements, the results can have musical worth beyond simple shaking, tapping, and playing on every beat.

Try to orchestrate so that different instruments come in at certain times and play different rhythms. More competent players can play melodies on xylophones and tone bells. For some tunes (those written in the pentatonic key), it is possible to create accompaniments of just two notes (a bordun) played over and over. More complicated parts can use as few as four notes (in 4/4 time) or three (in 3/4 time). These also can be repeated over and over. When several instruments are combined, the results can be quite musical. (See Chapter 1, sections IX, X, and XI for further ideas.)

It might be very difficult for some seniors to switch parts or instruments for the same song, although it might be possible for a different piece.

It is very important to choose instruments that are as "adult" as possible in sound and appearance. Go to a percussion supply house rather than an educational music company.

Singing Groups for Active and Well, and Fragile Seniors

When working with a singing group, try to cover as wide a variety of music as possible, from as many different eras as possible. The old "tried and true" sing-along songs as well as show tunes from later years are always popular with seniors. Many songs of recent years (excluding perhaps M.C. Hammer and heavy-metal music) can also be exciting for older people to sing. The group itself will, of course, suggest many tunes that they want to work with. Learning new lyrics is difficult, while singing songs that they learned many years ago will be easier.

1. Many older people love to sing children's songs and nursery rhymes. Perhaps these songs remind them of their childhood experiences, or those of their own children or grandchildren.

2. Work with themes – holidays, seasons, motor cars, different countries (perhaps those the participants come from), a special outing,
and so on. Themes can be developed with pictures, costumes,
special foods, slides, videos, posters, sound effects, and special
instruments. This approach helps to keep the program relevant
and to keep the individuals in touch with everyday reality.

3. Themes can also cover events in the past such as Friends,
Working Life, or Favorite Singers. Once started, the suggestions
will come thick and fast.

4. Using one special song, chant, and/or activity for the opening
and closing of each session gives a feeling of completeness and
helps avoid confusion.

5. Always start the singing session with warm-up vocal and breathing exercises.

6. Learn to play a portable, accompanying instrument such as a guitar, ukulele, Autoharp, or accordion. This allows you to move
among the group and to make one-to-one contact with individuals. It is very important to engender this spirit of personal contact.

7. Some facilities have had success with a karaoke night. Everyone
has an opportunity to sing solo with a recorded background
(instrumental and video) accompaniment.

Listening to Music

Listening to a variety of music on tape is very popular with seniors.
They will love to hear music of their childhood, music of their country of origin, or music that has been meaningful to them in their lives.
Music can help lift some of the fog they may be experiencing and
helps them be in the present even for just a short time.

People who are hard of hearing might profit from using Walkmans
or some other easily operated cassette player. Try to find one that has
fairly large controls and uses a knob to adjust the volume. Knobs are
familiar; "sliders" are not.

I recall a lovely lady of 95 who was quite disoriented and rather
deaf. She did not want to use her hearing aid because of the confusion
of noises she heard. When we put the headphones on and piano
music was played, her face lit up with pleasure. Waltzes, ballet music,
and Mozart were fine, but she told us she did not "like *that* much"
when the Bach cassette was played. This woman, by the way, still
played hymns and other music (by ear) on the piano every day.

If a person is bed-bound, use one of the small, flat speakers that fit
under the pillow. These work better than headphones in many cases.

BIBLIOGRAPHY

Basic Adult Piano Course, Levels 1 and 2. Sherman Oaks, CA: Alfred Publishing, 1983. One of the best adult piano courses available.

Bright, Ruth. *Music in Geriatric Care*. New York: Musicgraphics, 1980.

— *Practical Planning in Music Therapy for the Aged*. Sherman Oaks, CA: Alfred Publishing Co., 1984.

Caplow-Linder, Erna. *Therapeutic Dance/Movement: Expressive Activities for Older Adults*. New York: Human Sciences Press, 1979.

Douglass, Donna. *Accent on Rhythm. Music Activities for the Aged*. St. Louis, MO: MMB Music Inc. 1985. Contains many ideas for movement and music activities for senior citizens.

Hanser, Suzanne B. "The Future of Music Education and Therapy: Programming with Older Adults in the Community." *Music Education Facing the Future*. Proceedings of the 19th World Conference of the International Society for Music Education. Jack P.B. Dobbs, ed. 357–60. Helsinki, Finland: 1990.

The Last Days of Living. 16 mm film. National Film Board. Filmed in the Palliative Care Unit, Royal Victoria Hospital, Montreal, Quebec, this movie shows how music can help patients in the last days and hours of their lives.

Karras, Beckie. *Down Memory Lane and Moments to Remember*. Mt. Airy, MD: Eldersong Publication Inc.: 1985 and 1989. Excellent books with topics, ideas, and songs for working with groups in retirement and nursing homes.

— *With a Smile and a Song – Singing with Seniors*. Kensington, MD: Circle Press, 1988. Includes titles of hundreds of songs suitable for singing with senior citizens and others. Organized under topics such as Love, Shopping, Money, Seasons, and so on. Also included are ideas for making the sing-alongs more successful and some sample outlines for sessions. These titles are available through MMB Music Inc., St. Louis, MO.

Munro, S. *Music Therapy in Palliative/Hospice Care*. Stuttgart, Germany: Fischer Press, 1983. Available from MMB Music Inc., St. Louis, MO.

Munro, S., and B. Mount. "Music Therapy in Palliative Care," *Canadian Medical Association Journal* 119(9) (November 4, 1978).

Sing Out! A Collection of All Time and Old Time Favorites. Words and music (easy piano accompaniments) available from Gordon V. Thompson Music, 85 Scarsdale Rd., Suite 101, Don Mills, Ontario, Canada, M3B 2R2. Books containing words only, in large print for easy reading, are available from the Office for Senior

Citizens Affairs, 76 College St., 6th floor, Queen's Park, Toronto, Ontario, Canada, M7A 1N3.

Fake Books

Many titles are available in music stores. The melodies, lyrics, and chord symbols to hundreds of songs are given, allowing the user to create his or her own accompaniments on the instruments of choice.

10 BOOKS, RECORDS, AND TAPES

Alvin, Juliette. *Music Therapy*. Revised and edited by Auriel Warwick. London: John Clare Books, 1983.

Athey, Margaret, and Gwen Hotchkiss. *A Galaxy of Games for the Music Class*. West Nyack, NY: Parke Publishing, 1975.

Bartle, Jean Ashworth. *Lifeline for Children's Choir Directors*. Toronto, ON: Gordon V. Thompson Music, 1988.

Bastien, James, and Jane Bastien. *Bastien Piano Series*. San Diego, CA: Neil A. Kjos, 1985–87. Includes books for many levels as well as supplementary texts of performance pieces and theory. Some of the beginning books have colorful illustrations that might be confusing to students who have learning disabilities.

Bigler, Carole L., and Valery Lloyd-Watts. *More Than Music: Studying Suzuki Piano*. Athens, OH: Senzay Editions, 1979.

Birkenshaw, Lois. *Music for Fun, Music for Learning*. Third edition. Toronto, ON: Holt, Rinehart and Winston, 1983. In the United States, available from Magnamusic-Baton Inc., St. Louis, MO.

Birkenshaw-Fleming, Lois. *Come On Everybody, Let's Sing*. Toronto, ON: Gordon V. Thompson Music, 1989. A book with accompanying records or tapes on teaching music in the regular classroom, in classes with mainstreamed students, and in classes of students with disabilities.

Brown, Steven. *Successful Sounds Series*. A piano course designed to teach basic keyboard skills to students (children and adults) with special learning needs. 204 E. Woolcott, Harrisburg, IL, 62946.

Celebration Series. Royal Conservatory of Music, Toronto. Published by The Frederick Harris Music Co. Ltd., Oakville, ON: 1990. A graded series of music from grades I to VIII piano. Includes a *Study Guide Series*, comprising books of studies and cassette tapes of all the pieces and studies in the series played by the performing artist faculty of the Royal Conservatory.

A Different Understanding. Toronto: TVOntario, 1981. A TV series on helping children with special needs. Includes the following background booklets: Autism, Delayed Language Development, Learning Disabilities, and Normal Needs of Children with Disabilities.

Gardner, Howard. *Cognitive Approach to Learning*. New York: Basic Books, 1982.

— *Frames of Mind: The Theory of Multiple Intelligences*. New York: Basic Books, 1983.

Hammond, Susan. *Beethoven Lives Upstairs, Mozart's Magic Fantasy, Mr. Bach Comes to Call*, and *Vivaldi*. Toronto, ON: Classical Kids 1988–1991. Four recordings that are excellent for introducing children of all ages, and adults too, to classical music. *Beethoven Lives Upstairs* is available on video (A Divine Videoworks Production, 1992).

Hanser, Suzanne B. *Music Therapist's Handbook*. St. Louis, MO: Warren H. Green, 1987. An excellent overview of music therapy, detailing its use with many special populations.

Herman, Fran, and James C. Smith. *Accentuate the Positive*. Toronto: Jimani Publications, 1988. A helpful book about working with children who have physical disabilities using music, art, and drama.

Hoenak, Peg. *Let's Sing and Play*. Book 1. Bethesda, MD: Music Works, 1986. A recorder method that begins by using letter names for the notes.

Homespun Tapes. Woodstock, NY. Lessons for many different instruments on audio and/or video tape for all levels – from beginner to professional – in folk, blues, jazz, pop and classical music.

Keetman, Gunild. *Elementaria*. Translated by Margaret Murray. London: Schott and Co., 1974. The most complete description of the Orff approach to music education.

Kemp, Helen. *Helen Kemp on Junior Choirs*. Dayton, OH: Lorenz, 1962.

Konowitz, Bert. *Music Improvisation as a Classroom Method*. New York: Alfred Publishing, 1973. Contains many ideas to stimulate creativity.

Krout, Robert. *Teaching Basic Guitar Skills to Special Learners*. St. Louis, MO: Magnamusic-Baton, 1983.

Lee, Dennis. *Alligator Pie, Garbage Delight, The Ice Cream Store, Jelly Belly*, and other titles. Toronto, ON: Macmillan; HarperCollins, 1974–1991. Wonderful poems to capture the imagination of children.

Levin, Gail and Levin, Herbert. *Learning through Music*. Boston: Houghton Mifflin Company, 1974.

Mel Bay Publications. Pacific, MO. A selection of method books, cassettes, videos, and song collections for the professional and amateur alike. Some, such as the "Fun With ..." series, cover every conceivable instrument from viola to penny whistle. The "You Can Teach Yourself" series is excellent for the older student and also includes cassettes. Mel Bay publications can be obtained in Canada at music stores or through Warner/Chappell Music Canada Ltd.

Mofson, Sheila. *Shapes and Sounds: A Unique Approach to Reading Piano Music*. Syracuse, NY: Self-published, 1984.

Music Minus One. 50 S. Buckhout St., Irvington, NY, 10533. Tapes include just the accompaniment; the solo part is to be played by the student.

Nordoff, Paul, and Clive Robbins. *Music Therapy in Special Education*. St. Louis, MO: Magnamusic-Baton, 1985.

Orff, Gertrude. *The Orff Music Therapy*. London: Schott and Co., 1980.

Orr, Hugh. *Basic Recorder Technique*. Toronto, ON: Berandol Music, 1961.

Pace, Robert. *Music for the Piano* (revised). New York: Lee Roberts, 1975–1985. A series that uses the multiple-key approach.

Palmer, Willard, Morton Manus, and Amanda Vick Lethco. *Alfred's Basic Piano Library*. Sherman Oaks, CA: Alfred Publishing, 1981–1988. Includes many basic piano teaching books for young learners and also the *Basic Adult Course*, Levels 1 and 2. These books use the gradual, multiple-key approach.

Peterson, Meg. *The Complete Book for Autoharp or Chromaharp*. Pacific, MO: Mel Bay Publications, 1980.

Rohrbough, Lynn, and Cecilia Riddell. *Handy Play Party Book*. Burnsville, NC: World Around Songs Inc., 1983. A small book filled with excellent folk songs and dances.

Rubin, Mark, and Alan Daniel. *The Orchestra*. Toronto, ON: Douglas and McIntyre, 1984. This book accompanies a wonderful recording narrated by Peter Ustinov.

Sacks, Oliver. *The Man Who Mistook His Wife for a Hat*. London: Picador-Pan Books, 1980.

— *A Leg to Stand On*. London: Picador-Pan Books, 1986. Both of the above books by Oliver Sacks tell about the healing powers of music.

Schulberg, Cecilia. *The Music Therapy Sourcebook*. New York: Human Science Press, 1981.

Silini, Flora. *Experiencing Music with the Piano*. A Method for Teaching the Mentally Handicapped. Lawrence, KS: Self-published, 1981. This book gives many ideas and techniques for teaching piano to special-needs students. Unfortunately, it is out of print and difficult to obtain.

Smith, Corinne Roth. *Adapting Piano Instruction to the Needs of Children with Learning Disabilities: Merging Research and Intervention.* Reston, VA: ERIC Clearinghouse on Handicapped and Gifted Children, The Council for Exceptional Children, 1987.

Smith, Corinne Roth, and Sheila Mofson. "Adapting Piano Instruction." *Teaching Exceptional Children* 20(3) (Spring 1988): 22–25.

Suzuki, Shinichi. *Nurtured by Love.* Translated by Waltraud Suzuki. Smithtown, NY: Exposition Press, 1983.

Suzuki Piano School Vols. 1 and 2. Tokyo: 1978. Distributed in the United States by Summy-Birchard/Warner Bros., Secaucus, NJ.

Walther, Tom. *Make Mine Music.* Boston: Little, Brown and Company, 1981. This book has excellent ideas for making and playing instruments. It also includes chapters on sound – how it is produced by different instruments and other means. Also contains information on orchestral instruments.

Warren, Jean. *Piggyback Songs* and *More Piggyback Songs.* Everett, WA: Totline Press, Warren Publishing House. P.O. Box 2255, Everett, WA, 98203

Wilson, Frank. *Tone Deaf and All Thumbs?* New York: Vintage Books, 1987.

11 USEFUL ADDRESSES

GENERAL

American Association for Music Therapy, P.O. Box 27177, Philadelphia, PA, USA, 19118.

British Society for Music Therapy, Guildhall School of Music and Drama, Barbican, London, England, EC2Y 8DT.

Canadian Association for Music Therapy (CAMT) / Association de Musicothérapie du Canada (AMC), P.O. Box 2132, Sarnia, ON, Canada, N7T 7L1.

National Association for Music Therapy, 505 11th Street, SE, Washington, DC, USA, 20003.

National Music and Disability Information Service, c/o Dartington College of the Arts, Totnes, Devon, England, TQ9 6EJ. This service offers information on the many music programs for people who have disabilities in Great Britain. Has also developed over 16 resource papers on various disabilities.

MENTAL DISABILITIES

American Association of Mental Retardation, 1719 Kalorama Rd., NW, Washington, DC, USA, 20009.

British Institute of Mental Handicap, Stourport House, Stourport Rd., Kiderminster, Worcs., England, DY11 7QG.

Canadian Association for Community Living / Association canadienne pour l'intégration communautaire, Kinsman Building, York University, North York, ON, Canada, M3J 1P3.

PHYSICAL DISABILITIES

Canadian Cerebral Palsy Association / Association canadienne de paralysie cérébrale, 880 Wellington Street, Suite 612, Ottawa, ON, Canada K1R 6K7

Epilepsy Canada / Épilepsie Canada, 1470 rue Peel, Suite 745, Montréal, Québec, Canada H31 1T1.

Epilepsy Foundation of America, 4351 Garden City Dr., Landover, MD, USA, 20785.

Muscular Dystrophy Association, Inc., 3561 E. Sunrise Dr., Tucson, AZ, USA, 85718.

Muscular Dystrophy Association of Canada / L'Association canadienne de la dystrophie musculaire, 150 Eglinton Ave. E, Toronto, ON, Canada, M4P 1E8.

The Spastics Society, 12 Park Cresc., London, England, W1N 4EQ.

United Cerebral Palsy Association, 66 East 34th St., New York, NY, USA, 10016.

The Wheelchair Dance Association, 15 Knightsbridge Rd., Deckmont, W. Lothian, Scotland.

VISUAL DISABILITIES

The American Printing House for the Blind, P.O. Box 60885, Louisville, KY, USA, 40206. Has brailled scores and large-print music available.

The Association for Education of the Visually Handicapped, 711 14th St., NW, Washington, DC, USA, 20005.

Canadian National Institute for the Blind (CNIB) / L'Institut national canadien pour les aveugles, 1929 Bayview Ave., Toronto, ON, Canada, M4G 3E2. Has many brailled scores and books and tapes on music. The CNIB's Music Library will also transcribe music scores on request – depending on the availability of music braille volunteers.

National Library Services for the Blind and Physically Handicapped – Music Section. Library of Congress, Washington, DC, USA, 20542. Has material for loan including brailled scores, large-print material, music books, and periodicals (brailled) as well as music courses on cassette tapes.

Royal National Institute for the Blind, 224 Gt. Portland St., London, England, W1N 6AA.

HEARING DISABILITIES

Canadian Hearing Society / La Société canadienne de l'ouïe, 271 Spadina Rd., Toronto, ON, Canada, M5R 2V3.

Gallaudet University, Kendall Green, 800 Florida Ave. N.E., Washington, DC, USA, 20002. The only university for deaf students. Has an active music department, a good library, and good resource material.

LEARNING DISABILITIES

Learning Disability Association (ALD), 4156 Library Rd., Pittsburgh, PA, USA, 15234.

Learning Disability Association / Troubles d'apprentissage association canadienne, Maison Kildare House, 323 Chapel St., Ottawa, ON, Canada, K1N 7Z2.

AUTISM

Autism Society Canada / Société canadienne de l'autisme, 45 Sheppard Ave. East, Suite 304, North York, ON, Canada, M2N 5W9.

Autistic Society of America, 8601 Georgia Ave., Silver Spring, MD, USA, 20910.

Geneva Centre, 111 Merton St., 4th floor, Toronto, ON, Canada, M4S 3A7.

National Society for Autistic Children, 1A Golders Green Rd., London, England, NW11.

BEHAVIORAL DISORDERS

Canadian Mental Health Association / L'Association canadienne pour la santé mentale, 2160 Yonge St., Toronto, ON, Canada, M4S 2Z3.

MIND, National Association for Mental Health, 22 Harley St., London, England, W1N 2ED.

National Institute of Mental Health, 5600 Fishers Lane, Rockville, MD, USA, 20857.

SENIORS

Office for Senior Citizens' Affairs, 76 College St, 6th Floor, Queen's Park, Toronto, ON, Canada, M7A 1N3.

■

MATERIALS, BOOKS, AND RECORDINGS

Dorothy Dykma, 604 North Allyn, Carbondale, IL, USA, 62901. For *They Shall Have Music*.

Easy Hearing Music, Inc., P.O. Box 6347, Evanston, IL, USA, 60204.

Offers acoustically altered recordings for people who are hard of hearing.

Empire Music, Box 58116, Vancouver, BC, Canada, V6P 6C5. Toll-free number: 1-800-663-5979. Has a wide range of music and instruments including the easy-to-play Handchimes.

Frederick Harris Music Co., Ltd., 529 Speers Rd., Oakville, ON, Canada, L6K 2G4.

Gordon V. Thompson Music, A division of Warner/Chappell Music Canada Ltd. (see Warner/Chappell entry on page 121).

Guitar School for the Blind, 25557 N. Acenida Frasca, Valencia, CA, USA, 91355.

Homespun Tapes, Box 694, Woodstock, N.Y., USA, 12498. This company sells many audio and video tapes of lessons on teaching folk, blues, jazz, pop, and classical music on a variety of instruments and for all levels.

MMB Music (Magnamusic Baton), 10370 Page Industrial Blvd., St. Louis, MO, USA, 63132. Phone orders: 1-800-543-3771. Has the most complete list of books and materials regarding music and people with special needs. Offers large picks and other aids for playing instruments. Lists of books about the other arts are also included. When trying to locate any of these books, start with MMB Music. Ask for their catalogue, *Creative Therapy*.

Music Education Systems. 225 Major Mackenzie Dr. E., #624, Richmond Hill, ON, L4C 8T4. Phone (416) 460-7413.

Music Minus One, 50 S. Buckhout St., Irvington, NY, USA, 10533. Records of orchestral and other accompaniments with the solo part removed. The solo is played by the student.

Musik Innovations, Box 1, Alison Park, PA, USA, 15101. Phone orders: 1-800-677-8863. Many publications, some for people with special needs.

National Music and Disability Information Service, c/o Dartington College of the Arts, Totnes, Devon, TQ9 6EJ.

Onondaga Music Co. Inc., 412 South Clinton St., Syracuse, NY, USA, 13202. *Shapes and Sounds* piano music course by Sheila Mofson.

Piano Playhouse, P.O. Box 54157, Tulsa Oklahoma, USA, 74155. Gale Pederson has developed several courses on audiotape that are useful in working with the visually impaired and others such as people with autism and learning disabilities. Two of these are *Key to the Keys* and *Easiest Way to Improvise*. Accompanying large-print materials will shortly be published.

Royal Conservatory of Music, Toronto. 273 Bloor St. West, Toronto, ON, Canada M5S 1W2. Offers the Conservatory Music Rack, a sturdy, cardboard rack that hangs from the piano's music rack, bringing the music closer. Ideal for the young student or for those who have special needs.

Schott and Co., 48 Great Marlborough St., London, England, W1V 2BN. Has many music publications, especially materials for Orff, Music for Children. Schott also sells a recorder that is adapted for playing with one hand.

Schulmerich Carillons, Inc., 1767 Carillon Hill, Sellersville, PA, USA, 18960. This company will provide information on the use of handbells for people who have special needs.

Warner Bros. Publications Inc., 265 Secaucus Rd., Secaucus, NJ. USA, 07096-2037. Phone toll-free (in the U.S.) 1-800-638-0005 or (201) 348-0700. Has an extensive list of music of all kinds including Suzuki and Summy-Birchard publications as well as a comprehensive list of popular music.

Warner/Chappell Music Canada Ltd., 85 Scarsdale Rd., Suite 101, Don Mills, ON, Canada M3B 2R2. Phone toll-free 1-800-268-7736 (Canada) or 1-800-268-7846 (Ontario). Carries a complete line of music including the Gordon V. Thompson Music choral series and educational books, Suzuki texts, the entire Mel Bey catalogue, Summy-Birchard publications, Francis Clarke Piano series, Alfred Piano series, and many others.

Waterloo Music Co., 3 Regina St., Waterloo, ON, Canada N2J 4A5. Music books and Orff instruments. Also carries the Music Education Systems material.

NOTES

NOTES

NOTES